1

Introduction to THEATRE ARTS

VOLUME ONE / SECOND EDITION

STUDENT WORKBOOK

Suzi Zimmerman

Introduction to THEATRE ARTS

VOLUME ONE / SECOND EDITION

STUDENT WORKBOOK

Suzi Zimmerman

MERIWETHER PUBLISHING
A division of Pioneer Drama Service, Inc.
Denver, Colorado

Meriwether Publishing
A division of Pioneer Drama Service, Inc.
PO Box 4267
Englewood, CO 80155

www.pioneerdrama.com

Editor: Debra Fendrich
Project Manager and text design: Lori Conary
Cover design: Melissa Nethery

Printed in the United States of America
Second Edition

ISBN 978-1-56608-262-4

5 6 7 26 27 28

"Though this be madness, yet there is method in't."
(Hamlet II. ii.)

SPECIAL THANKS
to those who took the time to share their thoughts about theatre education, their memories, their expertise, and their love of the arts. I appreciate each and every one of you! Thank you to Kailee Graves, Carissa Thompson, Tanya Glover, Samantha Mitchell, Alicia Hooper, Molly Grogan, Amanda Lynn, Will Johnson, Devin Dusek, Rosemary Frederickson, Meg Schramm, Patty Harrison, and Darin Baker.

A very special thank you to former colleague Greg Arp* for your modern and insightful additions to our technical theatre chapter. You are a force in theatre, and I am honored to have your assistance and your expertise!

And another huge thank you to former student Rachel DeRouen. You were a star when you were in seventh and eighth grades, and you continue to make me proud today. This is why I teach!

* Greg Arp is the Coordinator for Speech and Theatre for Plano ISD and the 2012 PISD Secondary Teacher of the Year. He serves as an adjudicator for the University Interscholastic Leagues One Act Play Contest.

A DOZEN YEARS AGO,
there was a student who always came to my room after the 3:30 bell to tell me goodbye. My room was at the end of a long hall, nowhere near the student exit. She went out of her way to visit every day, spreading her joy, ensuring her teachers had smiles at the end of each day.

She participated in every play and every special event. If a set piece needed to be constructed at home, she was always part of the team volunteering to do it. She was also extremely energetic and sometimes needed to be reminded that it was time to listen, not talk. But those times were rare, and she was quick to smile an apologetic, sweet smile. And it is that smile—tinged with a hint of mischievousness—that I will always remember.

Brenna lost her ten-year battle with cancer long before she was able to see all the shows and build all the props and smell all the wonderfully musty old theatres. But did she try! She was just 26 and had fought the disease her entire adult life, but despite it, she continued to live, explore, and shine.

While cleaning out some old keepsakes, I found a card from Brenna thanking me for being her teacher and director. It was signed, "I love you, Ms. Z." It reminded me of how she would say goodbye at the end of each long, difficult day. She was the little voice that continued to whisper, "This is why you teach. This is why nothing is ever impossible."

I love you, too, Brenna. Rest peacefully.

Ms. Z

CONTENTS

CHAPTER 4 — ACTING

CHAPTER 5 — CHARACTERIZATION

CHAPTER 6 — PUBLICITY AND OTHER PRODUCTION BUSINESS

CHAPTER 7 — PLAY PRODUCTION

CHAPTER 8 — THEATRE HISTORY

CHAPTER 9 — GAMES AND IMPROVISATION

CHAPTER 10 — PLANNING FOR THE FUTURE

CHAPTER 1

GETTING STARTED

THE THEATRE FAMILY

Are You Ready for the Stage?
Getting To Know You Bingo

EXPECTATIONS

Rehearsal, Performance, and Classroom Expectations
Bell Work

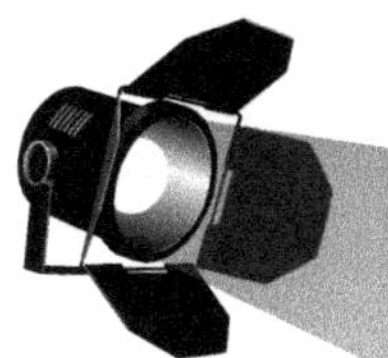

THE THEATRE FAMILY

While it is truly impossible to pinpoint, it is likely that acting had its beginnings in the days of cavemen. Scholars believe that kills were re-enacted for the tribe by hunters in the light of campfires. What followed was likely a slow evolution in storytelling, the passing down of history, religious and fable sharing, and news broadcasting. Eventually, troupes of actors would travel from town to town performing on wagons converted into stages. They would live as families, but women would not act for many years. Still today, performing (and the arts, in general) tend to be a family affair. Sometimes performing parents bring their young children to the set because the hours are long, and this is one way they can spend time with each other. Thus, young family members' love of the arts are imprinted from a young age.

Even when they are not related, cast members spend an extraordinary amount of time together. They share emotions and act out situations that are generally reserved for their closest friends and family. Can you imagine the difficulty of acting like you are in love with someone you barely know? It would be equally difficult to realistically portray hatred if the actor standing opposite you is a complete stranger or your best friend.

Cast members also count on each other to deliver their cue lines, use proper stage combat methods, and to be prepared. In the event that one feels another is falling short of their duties, the two will need to resolve their problems. All of this is more effective when the cast knows and likes one another versus a group of strangers or a situation where there is hostility. When you do scenes in class, you and your partner or group are a cast, so this also applies to you as a theatre student.

For young actors who are just getting started, knowing their classmates who will one day be their audience is also vital. Acting is very personal, and a great deal of teamwork, trust, and support are needed. Student actors stand in front of their classmates, allowing them to watch and listen, judge, and critique their performance. The stories in scene work are interesting because they explore emotions and situations not found in everyday life. While this makes a scene entertaining for the audience, it can be intimidating to inexperienced actors. Why?

First, each of us has certain emotions we are comfortable sharing with anyone and others we find more private—sadness, for example. By exposing these private emotions in front of our peers, we are letting them see us as more vulnerable. Second, many fear criticism and failure.

There are a number of reasons why performing can be a frightening experience, but there is also a simple solution. Actors must become a team—almost like a family. To start, the teacher and class will learn as much as they can about one another. Ground rules for what is acceptable before, during, and after performances are clearly defined so everyone feels safe. Finally, trust and dependability are developed so that performances are approached with eager anticipation rather than nervousness. Once the teacher is confident that each student is ready to be a respectful audience member and a dependable partner, performances may begin.

NAME ______________________________ PERIOD ______ DATE __________

ARE YOU READY FOR THE STAGE?

How would you feel acting out each emotion, characteristic, or action onstage as part of your scene?

0 = WOULD NOT DO

1 = VERY UNCOMFORTABLE

2 = SOMEWHAT UNCOMFORTABLE

3 = COMFORATABLE

_____ HYSTERICAL
_____ REVERENT
_____ FRIGHTENED
_____ CHILDISH
_____ ANGRY
_____ PAINED
_____ EVIL
_____ DITZY

_____ JOYOUS
_____ DEPRESSED
_____ IN LOVE
_____ HATEFUL
_____ CRYING
_____ LONELY
_____ ECSTATIC
_____ HEARTBROKEN

_____ PARENTAL
_____ HANDICAPPED
_____ DYING
_____ MENTALLY ILL
_____ DRUNK
_____ SHAKESPEAREAN
_____ STAGE FIGHT
_____ FOREIGN ACCENT

ADD UP ALL YOUR NUMBERS AND PUT THE TOTAL HERE: __________

62-72: You are ready to take on just about any role with confidence. You would probably make a good partner for those who score either high or low.

40-61: You are on your way to feeling comfortable in just about any role. With a little work, you will be a confident actor. The more comfortable you are with your classmates and stage partners, the easier difficult roles will seem.

18-39: You have a lot of reservations about acting, but you will be able to overcome this by becoming more familiar with the class. Start with a less challenging scene, and if you need a partner, choose one who will be supportive and whose comfort level is higher than yours.

0-17: Once you get to know the class and see others perform, your confidence level will rise. Choose simple scenes to start and talk to your teacher about tutoring. If possible, do not be one of the first to do your scene. Watch and learn from the other performers. You may be more ready than you think.

GETTING TO KNOW YOU BINGO

Talk to your peers and find someone who fits each of the traits in the squares below. Each of your classmates may sign your card _____ times. There will be a winner for the first row completed, the first X completed (from the four corners in to the center), for the first outer frame (all of the spaces on the outer edge of the card), and for the first blackout. Don't forget to ask your teacher to sign some squares. The center space is free!

I love to read	I have been on a crew for a play	I am good at history	I have been to an audition	I like to go to sporting events	I have more than three pets	I have never flown in an airplane
I do not like heights	I like action movies	I love to play video games	I do not watch much TV	I have been in a play	I am bilingual	I like to surf the internet
I like to take long walks	I write poetry or stories	I am quiet	I do not like unusual food	I am good at math	I am good at English	I have seen a live play
I do not care for social media	I plan to study theatre in college	I am a funny person	FREE	I am athletic	I like to care for people	I love the indoors
I like to go to the museum	I am artistic	I know someone famous	I ride the bus to school	I like to sing	I like to travel	I like to dance
I plan to go to medical school	I ate breakfast this morning	I plan to become a teacher	I do not have any pets	I have bungee jumped	I like to clown around	I like to swim
I plan to study law	I never eat breakfast	I walk to school	I love the outdoors	I get to school in a car each day	I am good at science	I am a serious person

EXPECTATIONS

Like any other instructor, your drama teacher has clearly defined rules and expectations and ensures they are followed in order to have a well-organized class. Even though theatre is very different from math, science, and social studies, the expectations are basically the same: complete the work when, where, and how the teacher instructs.

Likewise, rehearsals and performances have basic standards, starting with how to give feedback. While helping classmates iron out the wrinkles in a scene, find ways to improve the performance without being negative or hurtful. Rather than saying, "That looks stupid," you might say, "That's one way of doing it, but maybe you can try..." If you cannot think of a constructive way to give feedback, then it probably does not need to be said. You can avoid coming across as negative by following up with statements like "I like that much better," or "That's much more believable." Use tact when offering advice, and remember that there is more than one correct way of doing things.

While others are performing, be supportive and courteous. Do not make noises, faces, or quick movements that might be construed as an attempt to distract them. After their performances, if the teacher allows, clap heartily to show your appreciation.

Another standard for class performances is to be prepared *prior* to the first actor taking the stage. If you are performing, you will need your script (even though lines are memorized, it is traditional to have someone with the script offstage in case you need a line) and anything needed for the scene. If you are evaluating, you will need a pencil, evaluation forms, and anything else required in the audience (timers, recording devices, etc.). In a busy classroom, the sound of a backpack unzipping or a piece of paper crackling is hardly noticeable. However, when everyone is quiet and focused on an actor onstage, every little noise is magnified and can become a terrible distraction. Likewise, having everyone wait on you while you dig for your script can seem like an eternity. Do you want your audience to get impatient waiting for you before evaluating your performance?

Obviously, students should stay seated before, during, and after each performance to avoid distracting the actors and audience. Both you and the teacher should use the time between each group to fill out the evaluation sheet. The next group may use this time to set the stage for their scene.

The student sitting closest to the door will be designated as the one who needs to gesture to any visitors to wait until a scene ends before entering the room. It will also be helpful to have a sign laminated and ready to post on the door prior to each performance. However, there will be those—like a principal—who will ignore etiquette and enter anyway. Performers who are mid-performance should freeze and stay in character; they should not interact with visitors but should focus on where they are in their scene. As soon as the visitor is situated, the teacher will call "action" so that the performers may continue. This is actually a fantastic way to learn focus and concentration.

Having a positive and supportive performance environment is fundamental to any successful theatre arts classroom.

REHEARSAL EXPECTATIONS

Bring your script and a pencil every day.

•

Stay on task.

•

Work only in your group unless otherwise instructed.

•

Keep criticism respectful and constructive.

PERFORMANCE EXPECTATIONS

Be quiet and still.

•

Have supplies ready in advance.

•

Do not try to distract performers.

•

Be supportive before, during, and after performances.

•

Keep criticism constructive and offer it only when appropriate.

•

No one should enter or leave the classroom during a performance.

NAME ______________________________ PERIOD ______ DATE ______________

REHEARSAL, PERFORMANCE, AND CLASSROOM EXPECTATIONS

Rank the following scenarios 1 to 4 with 1 being the best solution and 4 being the worst. There is no right or wrong answer. Your teacher will discuss your answers with you.

1=BEST 2=SECOND BEST 3=THIRD BEST 4=WORST

1. Melissa is at the classroom door before she realizes that she has left her script in her locker. What should she do?

_____ She should turn around and go back to her locker even if she will be late to class.

_____ She should ask the teacher to allow her to return to her locker with a hall pass.

_____ She should try to find the book from which her scene came and write her lines out before rehearsal begins.

_____ If she has a partner, she should share a script with them and remember to bring her script next time.

2. You are completing a peer evaluation worksheet for duets. One group is not taking the assignment seriously and often breaks character. How should you phrase your criticism?

_____ "You are wasting the class's time."

_____ "That was a really funny scene. You made me laugh."

_____ "You two need to find other partners."

_____ "Maybe each of you should find partners who will complement you better and help you to be less nervous."

3. A visitor approaches the door during performances but does not enter. Instead he waits quietly at the door.

_____ Stay focused on the performance in progress. When the scene is over, the teacher will attend to the visitor.

_____ Get up and go over to the visitor. Figure out what he needs quietly and assist him.

_____ Motion to the teacher that a visitor is at the door so that she can figure out what he needs.

_____ Tell Matt the office needs to see him so that he can exit quietly during the performance.

4. On one rehearsal day your duet partner is absent. What do you do?

_____ Work quietly on your lines and blocking without her. When she comes back, the two of you can get caught up.

_____ Work on homework for another class. You can study your lines later in that other class since you will be caught up.

_____ Assist another group with their scene. You can prompt them, help them with their blocking, and give them direction when they request it.

_____ Wander from group to group trying to distract them. This is good preparation for performances since you never know what might happen. This will teach them to stay focused, and it will keep you busy during the rehearsal time.

BELL WORK

Your teacher may want you to complete a bell work or journal activity each day. They will instruct you as to when and how this is to be done. You should record your teacher's instructions here so that you may refer to them when needed. Bell work is located at the beginning of each section of this workbook.

- When will you be required to do bell work activities? ______________________________

  ____

- Remember that this is a time to work quietly.
- These "mini-lessons" are important. Each day's bell work is intended to introduce what your teacher will discuss in class on that day, or it will somehow connect with the planned activity.
- Remember, if you are absent, you must complete the bell work activity for that day along with any other missed assignments.
- The space provided should be just the right size to complete the bell work. However, if you need more space, you may wish to rewrite it in your journal, leaving a note reminding both your teacher and you of the whereabouts of the finished assignment.
- Your teacher may call on you to share your responses with the class.
- Make sure each entry is dated so that you can easily find each one and refer back to it when needed.
- Your teacher may use bell work questions as essay questions on tests or quizzes.
- Share your own unique ideas for bell work questions with your teacher. He or she may offer an incentive for your creativity. Spaces are provided on the last bell work page of each chapter for writing your suggestions.
- Write neatly, because these will be graded.
- When will your teacher require you to turn these in? ______________________________
- What else do you need to remember about completing bell work? ______________________

  ____

- Because responses are opinionated or theoretical, most teachers grade for completion rather than correctness. What will your teacher look for?

  ____

  ____

  ____

  ____

CHAPTER ONE NOTES:

CHAPTER 2
EVALUATION

DAILY BELL WORK—EVALUATION

UNDERSTANDING EVALUATION

Performance Evaluation 1
Performance Evaluation 2
Peer Performance Evaluation
Self-Improvement Plan
Movie/Play Evaluation
Script Report
Evaluation Test Review

NAME ______________________________ PERIOD ______ DATE ____________

DAILY BELL WORK - EVALUATION

Answer each question as your teacher assigns it, using the space provided. Be sure to include the date.

1. Date: ______________

   Why is it important to be evaluated?

2. Date: ______________

   Why is it important to evaluate your peers' performances?

3. Date: ______________

   Why is it important to evaluate yourself?

4. Date: ______________

   What do you predict will be the strongest areas of your performance? In which areas will you need improvement? On what do you base these predictions?

NAME ______________________________ PERIOD ______ DATE ____________

DAILY BELL WORK - EVALUATION

Answer each question as your teacher assigns it, using the space provided. Be sure to include the date.

5. Date: ______________

   What are some things the director will evaluate about the actors' performances in your class?

6. Date: ______________

   Define criticism in your own words. Can criticism be good? Explain why some is constructive and some is not.

7. Date: ______________

   When you see others' criticisms of your performance, what should you do?

8. Date: ______________

   What benefits might an actor get from recording their performance or voice?

NAME ______________________________ PERIOD ______ DATE ____________

DAILY BELL WORK - EVALUATION

Answer each question as your teacher assigns it, using the space provided. Be sure to include the date.

9. Date: ________________

   List some comments you might make about a performance if you did not care about the actor's feelings.

10. Date: ________________

    Phrase the above comments as constructive criticism.

11. Date: ________________

    If you knew your comments would be anonymous, how might they be different? Explain why this is.

12. Date: ________________

    Why is it important to plan the steps to making improvements? Can you think of other situations in which "improvement plans" are created?

NAME ______________________ PERIOD ______ DATE ________

DAILY BELL WORK - EVALUATION

Answer each question as your teacher assigns it, using the space provided. Be sure to include the date.

13. Date: ____________

    Many professionals are evaluated yearly before they can become eligible for raises or promotions. How do you think the prospect of receiving a larger salary affects their job performance?

14. Date: ____________

15. Date: ____________

16. Date: ____________

UNDERSTANDING EVALUATION

Evaluation is the way people feel about the quality of something. Before you buy a pair of shoes, you evaluate them. Are they a good value for the quality? Are they attractive? Are they comfortable? When you watch a movie, you evaluate it. Is the plot compelling? Are the actors believable? Does it hold my attention or resonate an emotion? Adults are evaluated at their jobs. Often, it is a formal evaluation that determines whether or not a professional will get a raise or how much that raise will be. A good evaluation may result in a promotion. When an actor performs, they are also evaluated.

Actors are selling a product that is difficult to evaluate early in their careers because it is based on an opinion. Actors are selling their talents. Many people think that talent is what you are born with. However, with training, actors can sharpen their skills so that the final product is a presentation the audience will enjoy. After the show, many actors anxiously await the reviews in the local papers so that they can read what the critics had to say about the performance. If the review is bad, the actor may be disappointed or angry, especially if they have no faith in the critic's taste. At the same time, actors' desire to perform well and improve daily will inspire them to take note of their weaknesses. When the reviews are good, actors will also take note of their strengths so that they may capitalize on them in the future.

Actors in training use many types of evaluations to learn their craft. Your teacher will use prior training and experience to critique you from an educated, mature point of view. Your peers will evaluate you from a more youthful point of view. And you will evaluate both yourself and your peers. By evaluating one's peers, you put yourself in the place of the critic and have the opportunity to learn even more. Many believe that self-evaluation is the hardest to do. Because we have been taught not to be "conceited," we have the tendency to cut ourselves down. However, knowing and capitalizing on personal strengths builds confidence, and that is one thing most successful people have in common: confidence.

The evaluations used for performances in this series of lessons have broken down the actor's craft into several small, manageable sections. In order to present the best possible performance, you must first know what is expected of you. The following descriptions summarize the information your teacher will use to complete the evaluation of your performances.

FOOD FOR THOUGHT...

Imagine a football player who is a great runner but can't throw very far. His coach says, "If you can improve your throw, you might make the team this year." The football player realizes that he probably lacks strength. He plans a strategy that includes several different muscle-building exercises for his arms while maintaining the program that made him a good runner in the first place. Within a few weeks, he sees a big difference and so does his coach. His hard work pays off when he makes the team. The actor can do the same thing. He must take the information he receives from his teacher and peers and plan a strategy to improve.

1. ***Approach***: Once your name is called, you should approach the stage or acting area quickly and with a quiet sense of enthusiasm to make a positive first impression. Many teachers will take points off for a student asking to go later for any reason, especially when their name has just been called. Furthermore, points may also be deducted for taking time to get out a script, getting a drink, talking to a friend, or having a negative attitude about the upcoming performance. Scene work is like being at an audition—behave like you want the job and are qualified.

2. ***Set-up***: If chairs or props are allowed for the scene, you should set up quickly and quietly, then find your starting place (the place where the first line will take place), and calmly wait for the audience's attention before starting. Your director will have their own standards for how this will occur. Some will require eyes to be closed briefly or heads to be bowed. Others simply request that the actor seize the moment and demand the audience's focus.

3. ***Introduction***: Many scene projects will start with an introduction. There are several types. A simple introduction includes your name and the character you will be portraying, followed by the title of the play and the playwright. These are more common in auditions. A creative introduction will give some backstory on the scene without explaining it, followed by your name, the character, and the title and playwright. Creative introductions are more common in scene competitions and lab work. Regardless of the style, the introduction must be said clearly and with confidence. Groups may do a group introduction or designate an individual to introduce the members.

   There are two types of introductions, informative and entertaining. An informative introduction is factual. State your name, the character you are playing, and the title and author of the play. An entertaining introduction gives some facts plus a little insight into the plot and is often creatively worked into the scene.

   - *Informative*—"My name is Edward Kinney, and I will be portraying the character of Mortimer from *Arsenic and Old Lace* by Joseph Kesserling."
   - *Entertaining*—"Aunt Abby and Aunt Martha were very sweet. What elderly gentleman wouldn't feel right at home boarding in their quaint old house and dining on their delicious home-cooked meals? So you can imagine their nephew Mortimer's surprise when he hears what became of kindly Mr. Midgely. *Arsenic and Old Lace* by Joseph Kesserling."

4. ***Energy***: Don't confuse energy with action. Even a quiet or sad scene must have energy. It may be vocal, physical, facial, or emotional. It may even be done with very intense eye contact. When you are energetic, your performance will appear enthusiastic, have appropriate movement and emotional levels, and will captivate the audience's attention, even during pauses between lines.

5. ***Voice:*** The voice is one of an actor's most important tools. As a matter of fact, we may never see many actors' faces, because they are voice-over artists—actors who mainly do commercials, radio, and animation. There are many qualities to a well-trained voice, but the main thing a director will look for is a mastery of projection, articulation, pronunciation, confidence, quality, and intensity. Other qualities a director may look for include a variety of levels of projection and/or dialect. For most scene work, actors will use their natural voices. However, becoming a professional voice artist requires actors to be able to manipulate their voices into unique characters—tones that aren't natural, like many of the unique cartoon voices.

   - *Projection* is the use of a voice that can easily be heard throughout the audience without seeming like shouting since the desired result is not always a voice that is loud. Try using a variety of levels of loudness while still projecting your voice across distance.
   - *Intensity* is the stressed tone of urgency or insistence in a voice, not to be confused with volume.
   - *Articulation* is to say the word and all of its sounds clearly.
   - *Pronunciation* is to say the word correctly. Sometimes words are pronounced differently depending on location or time period. Ask your teacher for help if you are unsure how to say a word.

> **Mastery** is the ability to successfully perform all parts of a task consistently and with little or no effort.

- *Quality* is the pleasantness of one's voice. Often this is not in the actor's control. Many people have physical reasons for not sounding "typical." It isn't always a bad thing, either. How many famous voices do you recognize the second you hear them because they are unusual? However, sometimes an actor's voice sounds odd because they use improper breathing techniques, use a "stage voice," or have a medical condition. Regardless, continuing to use poor speaking habits over a period of time could result in damage to one's voice or vocal cords.
- *Vocal confidence* is a combination of the projection, articulation, quality, and pronunciation. When you speak with vocal confidence, it sounds like you want to be heard. There is a naturalness to your voice, and the words flow in the way the character would speak.

6. ***Movement***: The use of posture, body language, gestures, blocking, props, business, and occasionally some pantomime that supports the goal of the scene is all part of what is collectively called movement. In college and in many acting schools, entire classes are dedicated to this. Have you ever seen a silent movie? Other than a few bits of written dialogue flashing up on the screen, the actors had to tell the entire story with just their hands, faces, and bodies. In modern theatre, the preferred style of acting is much more natural, but knowing what is natural for a particular character and being able to present that onstage may require some training.

- *Posture* is how you hold your body. There are many factors that can affect posture, such as age, health, the character's sense of self-confidence, and the character's relationship with others in the scene (or, in the case of a monologue, the unseen person to whom the monologue is directed). Social status, job, and the storyline may also play a part in the posture you adopt for your character.
- *Body language* is the message a character sends without speaking. It may include facial expressions, gestures, posture, movement, and even breathing. Think of a scary movie where the bad guy is chasing a young woman. The camera catches her hiding in a corner, pressed tightly into the small space, making her body as narrow as she can. She is practically holding her breath, tears streaming down her face, trying not to make a sound. Her eyes flicker back and forth, scanning the shadows for any sign of movement. Her entire body is racked with silent sobs, and her knuckles are white from the pressure of clutching the cinder block wall behind her. She hears footsteps. Her body tenses and her eyes widen. Her once-shallow breathing ceases. The footsteps approach even closer and stop just in front of her. We can't see who he is, but we can see her expressions give way instantly to the scrunched-up face of a sobbing child. She clutches her arms around her own body, sobbing uncontrollably, and allows herself—eyes closed—to slide down the cinder block wall behind her and onto the floor, curled up like a baby. Was the man the bad guy? Was he someone with whom she felt safe? No one ever said a word, but the body language told us exactly what was happening.

Food for Thought...

How do the blind learn body language if they cannot observe others using it? Is it an instinct with which people are born?

In 1995, researchers in Denmark conducted an experiment in which four people born blind were taught to use body language.

The project was such a success that now those born blind in Copenhagen, Denmark, are entitled to a free three-year course in communicating with body language.

Posture and body language are both very important in creating believable movement in your scene work. Equally important are gestures, blocking, props, business, and pantomime. While these are often considered inseparable, each is unique and will be factored into your evaluation. It is imperative that you understand what your evaluator will be seeking.

- *Gestures* are the movements you make with your hands to reinforce the message you are sending with your voice. For example, when your mother tells you to go clean your room, she may point in that direction to emphasize her point, even though you obviously know where your room is. Gesturing becomes more exaggerated when you are emotional.
- *Blocking* refers to the deliberate movements the actors make regarding where they are onstage and if they are sitting, standing, etc. Scenes need some movement to keep the presentation interesting. However, every movement must have a reason. Most scripts have the blocking written in parentheses or italics. Beginning actors generally follow these stage directions until they are comfortable blocking their own movements.
- *Business* is all of the little things an actor does onstage, in character, to appear naturally busy. It is intended to support the scene, not distract from it. The script will give clues as to which business would fit the character, but often the actor must read between the lines. For instance, when a girl brushes her hair during a monologue in which she is talking about her first love, the hair brushing is the stage business.
- *Props* are the things an actor uses onstage to carry out the requirements of the scene. For example, if the scene requires a character to take a drink from a cup, the cup would be a prop. Many teachers do not allow the use of props for scene work. Always ask the teacher or director before bringing props to class. Never bring toy weapons, fake cigarettes, or empty liquor containers to class for a scene.
- *Pantomime* is pretending to use props. Remember the girl brushing her hair above? Now imagine her brushing her hair, but without a prop brush. The action makes us think she is brushing her hair—the way she holds her hand as though there is a brush in it. Actors may also have to pantomime walking through doors, drinking from a cup, talking on a phone, or thousands of other things. They may still be delivering lines; it's just the stage business that is pantomimed without props.

> Mime is an art form characterized by men and women in white and black face paint, black pants, striped shirts, and bowler hats. While this is a stereotype, it should bring to mind a specific picture of this mime character "trapped in a box" or "climbing a ladder." Each movement is carefully and artistically per-formed in a slightly exaggerated fashion. On the other hand, pantomime is the act of pretending to do something without the benefit of props. Movements are mostly natural, as if the actor were really performing a task.

7. ***Facial Expressions***: Have you heard the expression a picture paints a thousand words? A single facial expression can do the same. Everyone probably remembers the picture of a young boy accidentally left home alone without adult supervision, mouth and eyes wide open, hands pressed squarely to each cheek. Expressions that support the goal of the scene are a vital tool. On the other hand, accidental facial expressions that tell the audience the actor made a mistake or forgot a line can ruin a good scene. Young actors must learn to cover their mistakes and not draw attention to them. Never allow an expression onstage that belongs to you—the actor—but does not fit the character.

8. ***Pacing***: Most stories follow a basic pattern. The beginning of the story, the exposition, starts slowly but at a steady pace and builds

in intensity toward the climax, the point of greatest action. After the climax, the story wraps up rather quickly in the denouement as it works its way to the end. (See figure.) Class scenes should follow the same basic pattern. They must have a beginning, middle, and end, and should progress at a rate that keeps them interesting and shows confident understanding and memorization. If the teacher has set a time limit, the scene must meet the requirements.

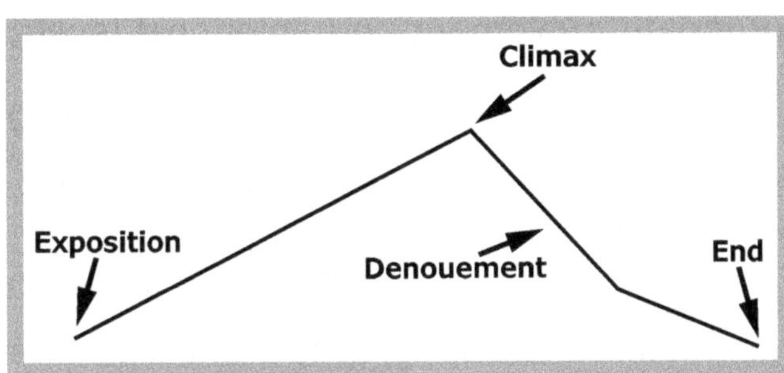

9. ***Characterization***: When doing scene work, young people are often timid about trying anything new. They are afraid of being judged by their peers. The characters in their scenes are reflections of the actors themselves. To make each scene unique and interesting, actors need to fully understand what the play and the characters are all about. Many actors even study the playwright to learn more about the characters. Once the actor is armed with details about the play, character, and playwright, they can portray a character who is fully defined and focused, has a unique personality, and uses emotions, body language, and vocal expressions that support the goal of the scene.

10. ***Focus***: A synonym for concentration, focus means to remain fully involved in the scene and to avoid being distracted by peers, visitors, sounds, mistakes, or calls for lines.

11. ***Closing***: Once the scene is over, the actor sits back down without commenting on the performance or making faces in order to make a positive last impression. The teacher may require a particular scene ending, such as a bowed head or the words "scene" or "cut." Ask your teacher what they expect for a closing.

12. ***Lines and memorization***: When performing, the scene should be memorized. However, occasionally forgetting a line early in the project is normal. To keep your performance smooth, give your script to someone who will prompt you loudly and clearly. When you forget a line stay focused and in character while trying to remember. If after a few seconds you still cannot remember, say "line," and your prompter will begin reading the line. Quickly pick up the cue and say the line from the beginning. Do not allow calls for lines to disrupt the flow of the scene. Ask your teacher if they count off when you call for lines and how many points each missed line is worth.

NAME ______________________________ PERIOD ______ DATE ____________

PERFORMER #______ CHARACTER ______________________________

PLAY/PLAYWRIGHT ______________________________

PERFORMANCE EVALUATION I

1. Introduction: Student states their name and the character, play, and playwright with confidence. Groups may do a group introduction or designate an individual to introduce the members.

   1 2 3 4 5 6 7 8 9 10

2. Energy: Performance is enthusiastic, has appropriate movement and emotional levels, and holds the audience's attention.

   1 2 3 4 5 6 7 8 9 10

3. Voice: Performance includes mastery of projection, articulation, pronunciation, confidence, and intensity. May also include a variety of levels of projection and/or dialect.

   1 2 3 4 5 6 7 8 9 10

4. Movement: The use of posture, body language, gestures, blocking, props, and business supports the goal of the scene. May include some pantomime.

   1 2 3 4 5 6 7 8 9 10

5. Facials: The scene includes appropriate facial expressions; the actor refrains from "making faces" when they become distracted.

   1 2 3 4 5 6 7 8 9 10

6. Pacing: The scene progresses at a rate that keeps it interesting and shows confident memorization; it meets the time limitations set by the teacher.

   1 2 3 4 5 6 7 8 9 10

7. Characterization: The character is fully defined and focused, has a unique personality, and uses emotions, body language, and vocal expressions that support the goal of the scene.

   1 2 3 4 5 6 7 8 9 10

8. Focus: Student remains focused on the scene and is not distracted by peers, visitors, sounds, mistakes, or call for lines.

   1 2 3 4 5 6 7 8 9 10

9. Closing: Student finishes scene and returns to their seat without commenting on the performance or "making faces."

   1 2 3 4 5 6 7 8 9 10

10. Lines and memorization: The scene is memorized, but the student is prepared and has given the script to someone who will call lines out clearly. If lines are needed, they are requested quickly and there is little disruption to the flow of the scene. Lines are worth ______ points each.

    1 2 3 4 5 6 7 8 9 10

BONUS POINTS FOR VOLUNTEERING:	Performer	Score	Minus Lines Missed	Plus Bonus	Final Score
5 points for the first volunteer, 4 points for the second, 3 points for the third, and 2 points for all other volunteers.					

NAME ______________________ PERIOD ______ DATE ____________

PERFORMER #_____ CHARACTER ______________________

PLAY/PLAYWRIGHT ______________________

PERFORMANCE EVALUATION 2

1. APPROACH AND SET UP

Timely 0 1 2 3 4 5

Confident 0 1 2 3 4 5

2. INTRODUCTION 0 1 2 3 4 5

3. ENERGY

Vocal 0 1 2 3 4 5

Physical 0 1 2 3 4 5

Emotional 0 1 2 3 4 5

4. VOICE

Projection / Intensity 0 1 2 3 4 5

Articulation and Diction 0 1 2 3 4 5

Confidence 0 1 2 3 4 5

5. BODY

Body Language 0 1 2 3 4 5

Gestures 0 1 2 3 4 5

Blocking 0 1 2 3 4 5

Movement 0 1 2 3 4 5

6. FACIAL EXPRESSIONS 0 1 2 3 4 5

7. PACING AND TIMING

Variation / Flow 0 1 2 3 4 5

8. CHARACTERIZATION AND EMOTION

Defined Character 0 1 2 3 4 5

Focused / Consistent 0 1 2 3 4 5

Believable 0 1 2 3 4 5

9. LINES CALLED CORRECTLY 0 1 2 3 4 5

10. CLOSING 0 1 2 3 4 5

BONUS POINTS FOR VOLUNTEERING:	Performer	Score	Minus Lines Missed	Plus Bonus	Final Score
5 points for the first volunteer, 4 points for the second, 3 points for the third, and 2 points for all other volunteers.					

NAME ______________________________ PERIOD ________ DATE ________________

PEER PERFORMANCE EVALUATION

Give specific information about each performance. You will be graded on completion as well as your ability to phrase comments constructively. Be thorough. ***Include a critique of your own performance.***

Performer	This performer was great at...	But could use a little more work on...
1.		
2.		
3.		
4.		
5.		
6.		
7.		
8.		
9.		
10.		
11.		
12.		
13.		
14.		
15.		
16.		
17.		
18.		
19.		
20.		
21.		
22.		
23.		
24.		
25.		
26.		
27.		
28.		
29.		
30.		

NAME ______________________________ PERIOD ______ DATE ____________

SELF-IMPROVEMENT PLAN

Answer each question honestly. Any honest answer will be given credit. This worksheet is intended to help you and your teacher analyze the success of the scene you performed in this class and to create a strategy for the next performance.

1. Character, play title, playwright:

____

2. *How* and *where* did you practice (both in class and outside of class)?

3. Did anyone in particular help you? Who was it and how did they help?

4. How much time did you practice outside of class?

5. Did you use all of the class time the teacher gave you? If not, what were you doing instead of practicing?

6. In what areas did you score highest from the teacher and what were some of the comments?

7. In what areas did you score lowest from the teacher and what were some of the comments?

8. According to your peers, what were some of your strengths?

9. According to your peers, where do you need to focus your efforts to improve?

10. In your opinion, what areas of your performance need the most attention?

11. What exercises or activities will you use to sharpen the skills that need improvement?

12. What can the teacher do to help you achieve success for the next performance? Is there anything you would like to have explained or taught again?

NAME ______________________________ PERIOD ________ DATE ____________

MOVIE/PLAY EVALUATION

Answer each question completely. Use a separate sheet if more space is needed.

Which did you see? *(Circle one)* MOVIE PLAY

Title: ______________________________

Director: ______________________________ Playwright: ______________________________ (if applicable)

Main Characters:	Actors:

1. What was the plot *(the storyline)*?
2. Most stories attempt to teach a lesson *(the moral)*. What lesson do you think this story was trying to teach?
3. What was the setting *(specifically when and where did it take place)*?
4. How did the set *(the buildings and scenery)* add to the play or movie?
5. What was your favorite costume and why?
6. What was your favorite special effect, sound effect, or lighting effect? Explain.
7. How did music add to the play or movie? Explain.
8. Was stage combat used? How?
9. What colors were used repeatedly? Why do you think the director chose these colors?
10. Who was your favorite character? Explain.
11. Did you like the movie or play? Explain.

NAME ______________________________ PERIOD ________ DATE ____________

SCRIPT REPORT

After you have read the play, answer the questions on this report thoroughly. You may have to do some research to find some of the answers.

Title: ______________________________

Playwright: ______________________________

Date published: ______________ Publisher: ______________________________

Other plays written by this playwright: ______________________________

____

What type of play is this? (Circle all that apply.)

Comedy   Tragedy   Historical   Classic   Full-length   One-act   Musical

Other: ______________________________

1. Where does the play take place?

2. What is the time period for the play?

3. List the main characters and tell a little about each of them:

4. What is the play about?

5. What is the climax of the play?

NAME ______________________________ PERIOD ________ DATE ______________

SCRIPT REPORT - CONT.

6. How is the conflict resolved?

7. What did you think of the play?

8. If you were in this play, which character would you be and why?

9. What is the theme or message of the play?

10. Find a line that you think supports the general theme of the play and write it here. Indicate the speaker, the act, and the scene.

11. Choose a character who undergoes a great change from the beginning of the play to the end. Describe the change and the impact it has on the course of the story.

12. What events led to the beginning of the play?

13. What do you think might have happened after the conclusion of the play?

14. Find several examples of symbolism and explain them.

NAME ______________________________ PERIOD _______ DATE ____________

EVALUATION TEST REVIEW

Fill in the blanks in each of the following clues, then find the word hidden in the puzzle. The number in parentheses indicates how many letters are in the answer.

1. Scenes should include a beginning, a ____________, and a clear ending. (6)
2. Actors will spend time ____________ their scene by carefully planning their movements. (8)
3. After a performance, actors should take their seat quietly and ____________ their performance. (8)
4. Actors begin defining their character with their ____________, or the way they situate their body. (7)
5. Articulation, diction, and projection are the main factors in clear ____________. (6)
6. Actors should strive to make their characters ____________, interesting, and believable. (6)
7. Actors must ____________ their voices in order to be heard by everyone in the audience. (7)
8. Students should be ____________ to take the stage with confidence and enthusiasm when their names are called. (8)
9. Knowing one's own strengths and being proud of them is ____________, not conceitedness. (10)
10. Good memorization will alleviate stage fright and ____________. (11)
11. Some actors mistake a lot of yelling and unnecessary movement for ____________ when all they really need is well-planned action, a dynamic voice, and appropriate body language. (6)
12. In most cases, actors should ignore minor ____________ from the audience and continue with their performances as normal. (12)
13. Body ____________ is the non-verbal communication actors must use to make their characters appear real and natural. (8)
14. A well-paced scene will be memorized, within the teacher's time limits, and will hold the audience's ____________. (9)

S	I	X	A	C	T	I	B	N	H	D	D	V	X	D
N	E	V	A	L	U	A	T	E	N	E	R	G	Y	I
O	W	L	P	O	S	T	U	R	E	R	A	E	P	S
I	P	R	O	J	E	C	T	V	G	A	E	S	E	T
N	A	T	T	E	N	T	I	O	N	P	H	T	C	R
I	F	V	E	U	Q	I	N	U	I	E	V	U	N	A
P	B	U	S	I	N	E	S	S	K	R	X	R	E	C
O	X	A	M	I	L	C	P	N	C	P	V	E	D	T
Q	W	E	E	X	N	E	V	E	O	M	O	S	I	I
S	H	T	G	N	E	R	T	S	L	A	I	D	F	O
P	A	R	V	C	T	O	X	S	B	N	C	N	N	N
E	X	O	H	L	A	N	G	U	A	G	E	A	O	S
I	M	P	R	O	V	E	M	E	N	T	S	H	C	X

15. Natural-looking ____________ will help the actors to reinforce their lines with their hands. (8)
16. Actors with good vocal confidence speak as though they want to be ____________. (5)
17. If good actors want to become even better, they will analyze their reviews to make ____________ (12)
18. Evaluating actors is difficult because critics must use their ____________. (8)
19. Hair brushing, writing, and hair twirling are all examples of stage ____________. (8)

CHAPTER TWO NOTES:

CHAPTER 3
SCENE WORK

DAILY BELL WORK—SCENE WORK

UNDERSTANDING SCENE WORK

LEARNING TO MEMORIZE

Whole-Part Memorization Practice
Part-Whole Memorization Practice

CREATING AN INTRODUCTION

Introduction Practice

REHEARSALS AND PERFORMANCES

Lab Scene #1 – Casey
Lab Scene #2 – Joey
Lab Scene #3 – Fatima
Lab Scene #4 – Nick
Lab Scene #5 – Pharrah
Lab Scene #6 – Jasper and Candy
Lab Scene #7 – Alix and Sam
Lab Scene #8 – Mira and Tam
Lab Scene #9 – Teacher and Taylor

NAME ______________________________________ PERIOD ______ DATE __________

DAILY BELL WORK - SCENE WORK

Answer each question as your teacher assigns it, using the space provided. Be sure to include the date.

1. Date: ________________

   Explain the process by which you will memorize or have memorized your scene.

2. Date: ________________

   Write out your scene in your own words.

3. Date: ________________

   Summarize your scene.

4. Date: ________________

   Why is good memorization important? Be specific.

NAME ______________________________ PERIOD ______ DATE ____________

DAILY BELL WORK - SCENE WORK

Answer each question as your teacher assigns it, using the space provided. Be sure to include the date.

5. Date: ______________

   Role score your character. Identify and explain their favorite color, food, and type of music or song. Also discuss their greatest fear, accomplishment, and ability. Finally, explain what got them to this point at which you begin the scene and where they will likely go after it is finished?

6. Date: ______________

   How are you like the character you portray in your scene? How are you different?

7. Date: ______________

   If you were to perform your scene tomorrow, what would it be like?

8. Date: ______________

   Why is trust an issue between duet partners? How might trust influence the cast of a play or musical?

NAME ______________________________ PERIOD ________ DATE ____________

DAILY BELL WORK - SCENE WORK

Answer each question as your teacher assigns it, using the space provided. Be sure to include the date.

9. Date: ____________________

   What are the things that need the most work before your performance?

10. Date: ____________________

    What do you like best about your scene? What do you like least? Explain.

11. Date: ____________________

    Attendance and behavior are vital in scene work and play production. Explain.

12. Date: ____________________

    What have you learned from your duet partner? What have you taught them?

NAME ______________________ PERIOD ______ DATE __________

DAILY BELL WORK - SCENE WORK

Answer each question as your teacher assigns it, using the space provided. Be sure to include the date.

13. Date: ______________

    Write a monologue from your character's point of view about a topic which has nothing to do with your scene.

14. Date: ______________

    Get with your duet partner and write a scene about being stranded on a deserted island. Each of you will write lines for the other actor to say. You must each have at least five separate lines.

15. Date: ______________

    Have you been happy with your performance so far? Why or why not?

16. Date: ______________

    Many teachers encourage students to attend acting competitions. How might this affect the way you rehearse your scene? Does competing appeal to you? Why or why not?

UNDERSTANDING SCENE WORK

When preparing a scene for a class project, it is important to fully understand the context of the scene within the play from which it originated. For example, if you found Maggie the Cat's famous speech from Tennessee Williams's *Cat on a Hot Tin Roof* in a monologue book, you might think it is just an angry speech from a jealous wife to her husband. However, if you read the play in its entirety, you will discover a desperate woman clinging to a love and a way of life that were never really hers to begin with.

The monologues and scenes in this chapter, however, are not from plays. They are called lab scenes, which means they were written specifically for you to experiment with and learn from. Each contains elements of theatre or acting that will help introduce you to scene work, acting, and the stage without being too overwhelming. Once you are comfortable with doing basic scenes like these, you may then select a more challenging scene, such as one from a play.

As you study each scene, keep in mind the evaluation your teacher will use to grade your performance. What kinds of elements will your teacher seek? They will look for you to approach the performance area enthusiastically and confidently. Your introduction must be well-prepared, as must your performance. They will also look for your scene to have good energy; but remember that energy does not always mean big and loud. It will be difficult for your teacher to judge any of this, however, if they cannot hear or understand you, so remember to project, speak clearly, and be confident in your delivery. Use the appropriate non-verbal communication such as body language, gestures, and facial expressions to support your spoken lines.

Another element your teacher will seek is realistic, believable movements that reinforce the lines. Good timing is also important. You may want to increase your rate of delivery or use pauses to keep the scene energetic and interesting. And most importantly, your teacher will look for signs of a well-developed, consistent, and believable character.

When your scene is finished, make sure you employ the type of closing your teacher requested. For example, some teachers require students to "drop" their heads as a sign that the scene is over. Others require students to say "scene." If a performance is completely believable, it is difficult to tell when it is over without the assistance of lights or sound, so be sure to ask your teacher how they wish you to end your scene.

One of the most important things your teacher hopes they will not notice in your performance is memorization trouble. When a scene is memorized to perfection, the actor will be completely focused on the performance rather than on which line comes next. However, if you are not one hundred percent confident on your memorization, that will be the main thing on your mind. Excellent memorization is the key to clearing the path to a good performance.

EVALUATION AND SCENE WORK...

You just completed the chapter on Evaluation. Now it is time to put what you learned to work by practicing and performing lab scenes. Use these clues to complete the list of elements your teacher will seek in your performances.

- E _ _ _ u _ _ _ _ _ _ c, confident approach
- Well-prepared _ n _ _ _ d _ _ _ _ _ _
- _ n _ _ _ _—not always big and loud
- Speak _ l _ _ _ l _ and co_ _ _ d _ _ _ _ y
- Appropriate body language, gestures, and f _ _ _ _ _ _ _ _ _ _ _ _ _ _ _ s
- Realistic m _ _ _ m _ _ _
- Good t _ _ _ _ g
- Well-developed _ h _ _ _ c _ _ r
- The teacher's required _ _ _ _ _ _ g
- M _ _ _ _ _ _ _ _ to perfection

LEARNING TO MEMORIZE

There are many ways to memorize. Many people have every song on their favorite radio station memorized. One reason is that songs are rhythmic and they often rhyme. These are two factors that make memorization easier. Have you ever had difficulty memorizing a series of items, but when the teacher put it to music, suddenly you were successful? Rhythm and rhyme are not normally a part of scene work; yet even if they were, most teachers and directors instruct actors not to rely on them.

Another reason why we memorize songs with little effort is that we hear them repeatedly. Repetition is often used in schools to assist students in memorizing a difficult series or long bit of information. Some actors can read a script a few times and have all of their lines memorized, even long monologues. This is the exception and not the rule.

Many songs are stories set to music. Knowing the events of the story is a third reason why songs are often easy to memorize. In acting and scene work, most experts will agree that knowing and understanding the events in a play is the best way to memorize it. This is called whole-part memorization. An actor using this process will need to know the entire plot and become especially familiar with what happens in the play just before and immediately after the scene to be memorized. They will also learn all they can about the characters involved. Often a character will have a hidden agenda in the scene, and if the actor is not aware of this, the scene will make little sense. It is extremely difficult to memorize a scene that you do not even understand. After an actor has completely researched the full play and characters involved, they may then need to read it aloud repeatedly until it is memorized. This requires a great deal of time even though much of the repetition is achieved in early rehearsals.

If repetition fails to work or if you cannot commit to the time-consuming process of whole-part memorization, you may wish to try a form of memorization less popular with professionals but often well practiced by students: part-whole memorization. In part-whole memorization, the actor breaks the scene down into smaller, more manageable chunks. These are memorized individually and then pieced back together bit by bit. While this is generally quicker, it is often used at the expense of fully comprehending the scene and its context within the play. As a result, performances may lack depth and characters may be shallow and lifeless, especially at first.

Discover which method or combination of methods works best for you. If the above methods do not produce positive results, try one of these suggestions:

- Record your lines and listen to them over and over again while going to and from school, when falling asleep, when you are getting ready for school, etc.
- Write your lines in a notebook. You may find that reading lines does little for memorization but that writing them helps with retention, especially if you say them aloud as you write them.
- Use creative devices for memorizing particularly challenging parts within a scene. For example, find a way to connect the last word of one line to the first word of the next line.
- If the scene is written in a difficult language or pattern, you may wish to try writing the scene in your own words and then converting it back into the language of the playwright.
- Once your scene is memorized, if you find yourself needing to peek at the same places repeatedly, you may wish to highlight those in a different color and spend more time working on just those spots.

WHOLE-PART MEMORIZATION PRACTICE

Write the exact time here: ________. Read the scene at the top of the page three times to yourself and then cover it. Write what you can remember on a separate piece of paper. Check yourself. How did you do? Now try reading it again out loud a couple of times. Again, cover the page and add what you can to your sheet of paper. Keep doing this until it is memorized. When you have the scene completely memorized and written out, put the exact time here: ________. How long did it take you to completely memorize this scene using whole-part memorization? Total time: ________.

CASEY: *(Brings MABEL a cup of hot tea.)* Careful. It's pretty hot. *(Starts to leave the room, but hesitates.)* Miss Mabel? I… Oh, never mind. Have you ever… *(Knocks over a broom.)* Oh, I'm so sorry. I am such a klutz! I'm just gonna go finish sorting the mail and then I'll leave. I'll see you tomorrow. *(Starts to leave.)* Miss Mabel… What's it like? *(Uncomfortable, but curious.)* I mean, to be blind? You must get lonely. I mean, I can see pretty good, but sometimes I feel like I am completely in the dark, you know what I mean? I mean, I know you do, but do you really? I have this friend, Victoria, and she's pretty nice. She's just about the only person I know who's not old enough to have great-grandkids! Oh, sorry. I mean, she's the only friend I have my age. Sometimes I don't even like her. Sometimes after we get together I promise myself I'm never gonna call her again or go to her house. But then, a few hours pass and I get so lonely, and I think that it's better to go to her house and sit around watching her smoke her dad's cigarettes and make prank calls than it is to be completely alone. I've never told anyone this, but… you won't tell, will you? One time she stole a CD from the gas station. It was some old singer from a long time ago, and she doesn't even have a CD player. She did, but her stepdad sold it. I didn't know she'd taken it until we were halfway home. She thought it was so funny! I was just mad and scared. I kept looking over my shoulder thinking the cops were gonna come get us. I was afraid that if I told her how mad I was, she would think I was a baby. You know, my momma may not be perfect, but she taught me right from wrong, and what Victoria did was wrong. It's not like she stole because she was hungry. She did it just for fun! That's the longest I ever went without calling her—a whole day! Miss Mabel… I… I never knew my grandma. My momma wouldn't have anything to do with her. She died about four years ago and my momma didn't even cry, wouldn't even go to the funeral. And you know I never knew my daddy, much less his momma. I would be very proud if I could call you my grandma… Would that be okay with you?

PART-WHOLE MEMORIZATION PRACTICE

Write the exact time here ________. Memorize the first line of the monologue and repeat it to yourself. Now memorize the second line. Once it is memorized, repeat the first two lines together. Continue to repeat this process until every line is memorized. Once the entire monologue is memorized, write it from memory on a separate sheet of paper and check yourself. How accurate was your memory? When you feel the scene is thoroughly memorized, write the exact time here ________. How long did it take you to memorize this scene using part-whole memorization? Total time ________.

JOEY: Darla's dad is this big writer guy. His name is Dwight—but that wasn't glamorous enough for the people that buy that stuff, so his pen name was Antonio Bishop. He wrote stories about this old guy who travels all over the world meeting beautiful women, but he never gets married because that would mean he'd have to settle down, you know? So Darla, she says to me, "Do you think he wishes he'd never had me?" She took it real personal, you know? Her mom had died a few years back, and Darla figured her dad had become almost like the guy he wrote about... except for the part about having a kid. So he bought her a fast car.

You know, my folks never went to college. My mom never even graduated from high school. They got married right after my dad graduated, so she dropped out. I was born the night she should have graduated. After that, having babies was her hobby! The night of the accident, she told me number seven was on the way... and that I'd have to spend less time with "that girl"... and that she was fed up being up to her ears in babies and no help!

So I left. My mom was standing at the screen door holding a screaming kid yelling at me to come back, but I just kept going. Darla picked me up halfway, crying so hard she could barely see, so I drove. Her dad said he wanted her to get away from me for a while, so he was sending her to boarding school in New York starting in the fall. We both cried, and I just kept driving. Neither of us said it, but we were leaving.

We were on Highway 12 by Pearl Lake. For the first time since we left, we were quiet. I looked at Darla and she tried to smile, but then she suddenly looked scared, and I realized I was headed off the road right toward the lake. I swerved and the car started spinning. There was a lot of screeching and screaming, and then we hit something and everything went black.

When I woke up, we were wedged against the cliff. Her head was against my shoulder. She was having a real hard time breathing, but I couldn't move to help her. I could tell she was in a lot of pain. I wished it was me, but I didn't feel anything. I couldn't feel a thing... I saw the flashing red lights and heard the sirens. I couldn't hear Darla breathing anymore.

All we wanted was to be happy. We just wanted to be together... happy.

CREATING AN INTRODUCTION

When you do scene work in class, your teacher may or may not have you do an introduction. However, you will need to have one in most competitions, auditions, or public performances. An introduction or slate is a short piece at the beginning of your scene that tells the audience who you are, who you are portraying, the play from which your scene comes, and its playwright. There are basically two types: informative and entertaining.

Even though it is very basic, the informative introduction is generally considered the preferred type for most scene work in class and at auditions. It is succinct and simple: "My name is Clifford Redding, and I will be portraying the character John in *Last Wrongs* by James Calidon." In duets and scenes with three or more people, one person will usually introduce the others, or each actor may take part in the introduction. Prepare your introduction in advance so that it is fluid and sets the tone for a well-performed scene.

Alternatively, your teacher may require you to do an entertaining introduction. Like the informative approach, it contains the facts about the scene, but this one becomes a part of the entertainment and is also the preferred type for competition. Again, it must be as well-prepared as your scene. It will give some of the same basic information as the introduction above, but it will also offer some insight into the plot. Although it is not done in character, it is done in the mood and tone of the scene. In other words, if your scene is tragic, your introduction must not be funny or happy. At the same time, you should strive to create a defined transition from the "actor" speaking to the audience to the "character" in the play.

Another thing that sets the entertaining introduction apart from the informative one is that it does not necessarily have to come before the dialogue, although it does need to be placed toward the beginning. Actors will often begin their scene, stop and step out of character, give their introduction, and then continue with their scene. It may be that they feel the content of their introduction works best if first set up with some dialogue. The dialogue from the scene that precedes the introduction is called a teaser. It gets the audience interested in the scene, teasing them into believing they can settle in to enjoy, when suddenly the introduction is inserted. By then, they are hooked.

The entertaining introduction is also more flexible than the informative one. Rather than saying, "I will be portraying..." an actor might say, "John lives in a world where..." to indicate his character's name. He will probably not say his own name. There is an unlimited amount of room for creativity, and the rule of thumb is that almost anything goes. Sometimes actors give background on the playwright or the era in which the play is set. Other times they may tell what happened just before this particular scene in the play. They might even quote a poem, compare the scene to a modern-day headline, or act as though they are in counseling and the audience is their "therapist." Introductions should never exceed one minute.

The following example of an entertaining introduction is written as dialogue for better clarity.

SAMPLE INTRODUCTION

[Teaser]

JUAN: *(As KELLER.)* Katie, I will not have it! Now you did not see when that girl after supper tonight went to look for Helen in her room—

SARAH: *(As KATIE.)* No.

JUAN: *(As KELLER.)* The child practically climbed out of her window to escape from her! What kind of teacher is she?

[Introduction]

JUAN: *(Out of character, turning to face AUDIENCE.)* Captain Keller and his young wife, Kate, were blessed with a beautiful, happy baby.

SARAH: *(Out of character, turning to face AUDIENCE.)* But when illness robbed their child of her sight and hearing, they were left with a girl who could not communicate. She lived in darkness and total silence.

JUAN: *(Out of character.)* But her world was far from quiet. There was a voice screaming in her head, fighting to get out. The Kellers needed a miracle.

SARAH: *(Out of character.) The Miracle Worker,* by William Gibson.

[Scene]

(Both students return to their characters and the scene continues on through the end.)

JUAN: *(As KELLER.)* I thought I had seen her at her worst...

NAME ________________________________ PERIOD ______ DATE __________

INTRODUCTION PRACTICE

Create an introduction for three of the Lab Scenes at the end of this section. Remember, some are monologues and some are duets. Your format for your introduction will be different depending on the type of scene. Include at least one monologue and one duet. One of your introductions may be *informative* while the others are *entertaining*. Refer to *Creating an Introduction* on page 41 if you need assistance. Create fictional titles for your scenes and use Suzi Zimmerman, the author of this workbook, as the playwright.

Lab Scene # ________ Informative introduction

Lab Scene # ________ Entertaining introduction without teaser

Lab Scene # ________ Entertaining introduction with teaser

REHEARSALS AND PERFORMANCES

Now it is time to get to work. You will begin rehearsing your scene, getting it ready for your first performance. Your teacher will give you details on their specific performance expectations.

Whatever time your teacher has allotted for you to prepare your scene, attendance is crucial. Ask your teacher in advance when they plan to conduct performances and write the date in your calendar. You will want to pace yourself accordingly. This guide assumes you will have five class sessions to prepare. Adjust it accordingly when planning your rehearsals.

Day 1—Rehearse your scene using your script. Mark ideas in the script using a pencil. Clarify any confusion early if you do not understand a word or a part of the script.

Day 2—Block your scene and write your blocking in your script in pencil. When will you sit? When will you stand and cross? Continue to work on memorization.

Day 3—Continue to rehearse using your script, but make it your goal to be doing the scene without the script by the end of this class period.

Day 4—Sit down and read your script again. Now that you have it basically worked out, it is important to make sure you did not miss anything, especially if you are working without a director. If you are required to use props, now is the time to work them in. Plan out your introduction and start practicing it each time you rehearse your scene.

Day 5—Have someone watch your scene and critique it, and do the same for them. Without arguing or defending your performance, thank them for their critique. You may now decide if you want to change anything based on their criticism. Spend the remainder of your rehearsal time polishing and perfecting your scene for performance.

How do you know when your scene is good enough for a performance? While the answer may seem straightforward, getting there and knowing when you are there may be more complex. Your scene will be ready for performance when it feels like second nature to you. In other words, when you feel like you could do it in your sleep, you are ready. It must be one hundred percent memorized, including lines and actions. If you are working with a partner, the two of you should be synchronized or almost instinctively paired in the scene. You also want to make sure that you are obeying the most basic rules of acting, such as projecting, remaining visible to the audience, and staying true to the script and the playwright's intent. Most importantly, the scene must have good energy throughout—even during silent pauses.

Now that you are ready, it's time to perform. Many teachers have their students perform scenes just once, while others prefer to see them twice, about two weeks apart. The benefits of doing each scene twice far outweigh doing them one time. For example, the audience and teacher will give the performers quite a bit of feedback after the first performance. Students should take that feedback to improve their scenes. Polishing scenes after a first performance is also similar to how actors polish a play after receiving feedback from the director. Finally, a perfected scene is great audition material, but few scenes are of that caliber after just one performance. Ask your teacher how many times you will perform your scene and record all the dates in your calendar.

LAB SCENE #1

CASEY, female, age 14

Casey has moved in with her great-aunt while her mother tries to get back on her feet after a third divorce. Her new neighborhood is on a quiet street with quiet, elderly people. Casey is the only one her age on the block. Sometimes she meets kids who are visiting their grandparents at the neighboring homes, but they do not stay long enough to become friends. Her only friend is a girl named Victoria, but Casey knows that it is only a matter of time before Victoria's bad choices get both of them into a lot of trouble. She has met Mabel, a kind, elderly blind lady who has asked Casey to spend an hour each day helping her around the house. The kitchen is tidy to a fault. She must be very careful not to rearrange anything, and she feels hopelessly clumsy.

CASEY: *(Brings MABEL a cup of hot tea.)* Careful. It's pretty hot. *(Starts to leave the room, but hesitates.)* Miss Mabel? I... Oh, never mind. Have you ever... *(Knocks over a broom.)* Oh, I'm so sorry. I am such a klutz! I'm just gonna go finish sorting the mail and then I'll leave. I'll see you tomorrow. *(Starts to leave.)* Miss Mabel... What's it like? *(Uncomfortable, but curious.)* I mean, to be blind? You must get lonely. I mean, I can see pretty good, but sometimes I feel like I am completely in the dark, you know what I mean? I mean, I know you do, but do you really? I have this friend, Victoria, and she's pretty nice. She's just about the only person I know who's not old enough to have great-grandkids! Oh, sorry. I mean, she's the only friend I have my age. Sometimes I don't even like her. Sometimes after we get together I promise myself I'm never gonna call her again or go to her house. But then, a few hours pass and I get so lonely, and I think that it's better to go to her house and sit around watching her smoke her dad's cigarettes and make prank calls than it is to be completely alone. I've never told anyone this, but... you won't tell, will you? One time she stole a CD from the gas station. It was some old singer from a long time ago, and she doesn't even have a CD player. She did, but her stepdad sold it. I didn't know she'd taken it until we were halfway home. She thought it was so funny! I was just mad and scared. I kept looking over my shoulder thinking the cops were gonna come get us. I was afraid that if I told her how mad I was, she would think I was a baby. You know, my momma may not be perfect, but she taught me right from wrong, and what Victoria did was wrong. It's not like she stole because she was hungry. She did it just for fun! That's the longest I ever went without calling her—a whole day! Miss Mabel... I... I never knew my grandma. My momma wouldn't have anything to do with her. She died about four years ago and my momma didn't even cry, wouldn't even go to the funeral. And you know I never knew my daddy, much less his momma. I would be very proud if I could call you my grandma... Would that be okay with you?

NAME ______________________________ PERIOD ______ DATE ____________

CASEY

Answer the following questions about the character, Casey, from Lab Scene #1.

1. What do we know for certain about Casey?

2. What do we know for certain about Mabel?

3. What do we know for certain about the setting?

4. What year do you think it is? Why?

5. What is the scene about?

6. Is the scene comic, dramatic, or a combination of the two?

7. What happened just before the start of this scene?

8. What do you think might happen after the scene if the story continued?

9. If this scene was from a play, what do you think it would be called?

10. What does Casey want in this scene?

11. What do you think Casey's hobbies might be?

12. If Casey repeatedly made a gesture in this scene, what would it be and why?

13. What color do you associate with Casey and why?

NAME ______________________________ PERIOD _______ DATE ____________

14. What object do you associate with Casey and why?

15. What animal do you associate with Casey and why?

16. In real life, would you be Casey's friend? Why or why not?

17. How is Casey like you?

18. How is Casey different from you?

19. What is Casey's most positive trait?

20. What is Casey's status in the world? Does she have money or power?

21. What does Casey fear and why?

22. Who does Casey admire and why?

23. What are Casey's parents like?

24. If Casey had one wish, what would it be and why?

25. What is your favorite line in the monologue and why?

26. Find ten words in Casey's monologue that you feel stand out as being the most descriptive of the overall purpose of the scene.

LAB SCENE #2

JOEY, male, age 17

Joey is a rebellious teen in a small town. His girlfriend got a car for her sixteenth birthday from her writer father, but she feared the mountainous roads, so Joey did all the driving. When their parents feel they are spending too much time together and pressure them to back off from the relationship, Joey and Darla take one last cruise along Highway 12. Afterward, Joey recounts his story in group therapy.

JOEY: Darla's dad is this big writer guy. His name is Dwight—but that wasn't glamorous enough for the people that buy that stuff, so his pen name was Antonio Bishop. He wrote stories about this old guy who travels all over the world meeting beautiful women, but he never gets married because that would mean he'd have to settle down, you know? So Darla, she says to me, "Do you think he wishes he'd never had me?" She took it real personal, you know? Her mom had died a few years back, and Darla figured her dad had become almost like the guy he wrote about... except for the part about having a kid. So he bought her a fast car.

You know, my folks never went to college. My mom never even graduated from high school. They got married right after my dad graduated, so she dropped out. I was born the night she should have graduated. After that, having babies was her hobby! The night of the accident, she told me number seven was on the way... and that I'd have to spend less time with "that girl"... and that she was fed up being up to her ears in babies and no help!

So I left. My mom was standing at the screen door holding a screaming kid yelling at me to come back, but I just kept going. Darla picked me up halfway, crying so hard she could barely see, so I drove. Her dad said he wanted her to get away from me for a while, so he was sending her to boarding school in New York starting in the fall. We both cried, and I just kept driving. Neither of us said it, but we were leaving.

We were on Highway 12 by Pearl Lake. For the first time since we left, we were quiet. I looked at Darla and she tried to smile, but then she suddenly looked scared, and I realized I was headed off the road right toward the lake. I swerved and the car started spinning. There was a lot of screeching and screaming, and then we hit something and everything went black.

When I woke up, we were wedged against the cliff. Her head was against my shoulder. She was having a real hard time breathing, but I couldn't move to help her. I could tell she was in a lot of pain. I wished it was me, but I didn't feel anything. I couldn't feel a thing... I saw the flashing red lights and heard the sirens. I couldn't hear Darla breathing anymore.

All we wanted was to be happy. We just wanted to be together... happy.

NAME ______________________________ PERIOD ______ DATE ____________

JOEY

Answer the following questions about the character, Joey, from Lab Scene #2.

1. What do we know for certain about Joey?

2. What do we know for certain about Darla?

3. What do we know for certain about the setting?

4. What year do you think it is? Why?

5. What is the scene about?

6. Is the scene comic, dramatic, or a combination of the two?

7. What happened just before the start of this scene?

8. What do you think might happen after the scene if the story continued?

9. If this scene was from a play, what do you think it would be called?

10. What does Joey want in this scene?

11. If Joey repeatedly made a gesture in this scene, what would it be and why?

12. What color do you associate with Joey and why?

13. What object do you associate with Joey and why?

NAME ______________________________ PERIOD ________ DATE ______________

14. In real life, would you be Joey's friend? Why or why not?

15. How is Joey like you?

16. How is Joey different from you?

17. What is Joey's status in the world? Does he have money or power?

18. What does Joey fear and why?

19. Who does Joey admire and why?

20. What are Joey's parents like?

21. If Joey had one wish, what would it be and why?

22. What do you think happened to Darla?

23. What is Joey's future like now?

24. What is your favorite line in the monologue and why?

25. Find ten words in Joey's monologue that you feel stand out as being the most descriptive of the overall purpose of the scene.

LAB SCENE #3

FATIMA, female, age 25

Fatima is the leader of the Sisterhood of Destiny, a club that preaches women's independence. She is having a hard time fighting off her urge to do the very thing she tells others not to do. She is getting ready for a rally and tries to practice her speech, pack boxes, and talk to her roommate all at the same time.

FATIMA: *(As though speaking at a rally.)* A woman is only independent when she is standing on her own two feet, paying her own way, and making her own decisions about education, career, and relation—oh! I almost forgot to tell you... I met the cutest guy! His name is Raul... He's Spanish. He's a buyer for a big Spanish department store, El Something-or-Other. He was in town for a big market, and I ran into him on the subway—literally ran into him—tripped over some lady's briefcase and pushed him right on top of a man with flowers. Daisies everywhere! But this guy, Raul, he just looks up at me and says, "Are you, how you say, all right?" He looked like an angel! He has these big blue eyes and eyelashes that just kept waving to me! I almost kissed him right there on the spot! Have you seen my enrollment forms? I had them right here on top of my *Live a Man's Life* book. Oh, look! Remember this? This is the Sisterhood at the first rally! Look, there's Alice and Breck and me and—ooh, gross! How'd she get in the picture? She married that writer who came to one of our meetings just so he could badmouth us in his column. The next day we had three members drop out, and we lost the support of the entire Lady Bikers Club! I heard she's already on her second baby, and do you know she quit her job? A woman is only independent when she is standing on her own two feet, right? Can you imagine being a housewife, not working, just spending the whole day with kids, gardening, cooking, *(Starts liking the idea.)* cleaning, shopping, taking care of Raul—I mean, your husband? *(Shakes the thought off.)* You know, I don't think my speech is passionate enough. Maybe I should say something about the male conspiracy to glamorize the... to disguise the role of the wife in a suburban setting as a desirable goal rather than the trap that it is. *(As a speech.)* Beware those who will shroud the position of the slave-wife in a veil of adorable little minivans, maternity clothes, and long walks in the park on sunny days, pushing the stroller, meeting other moms, not working. Not working. This speech is not working! *(Sits defeated, retrieving her clipboard from the seat.)* Enrollment forms! Found them. *(Takes a piece of paper and a cell phone from her pocket and punches in the number.)* Raul? Hi, this is Fatima, remember? From the subway? Yeah. That one. Listen, I've had a cancellation today and thought maybe you'd like to have lunch?

NAME ______________________________ PERIOD ________ DATE ______________

FATIMA

Answer the following questions about the character, Fatima, from Lab Scene #3.

1. What do we know for certain about Fatima?

2. What do we know for certain about the setting?

3. What year do you think it is? Why?

4. What is the scene about?

5. Is the scene comic, dramatic, or a combination of the two?

6. What happened just before the start of this scene?

7. What do you think might happen after the scene if the story continued?

8. If this scene was from a play, what do you think it would be called?

9. What does Fatima want in this scene?

10. If Fatima repeatedly made a gesture in this scene, what would it be and why?

11. What are some items Fatima might be packing for her rally?

12. What color do you associate with Fatima and why?

13. What object do you associate with Fatima and why?

NAME ________________________________ PERIOD ______ DATE ____________

14. In real life, would you be Fatima's friend? Why or why not?

15. How is Fatima like you?

16. How is Fatima different from you?

17. What is Fatima's status in the world? Does she have money or power?

18. What does Fatima fear and why?

19. Who does Fatima admire and why?

20. What are Fatima's parents like?

21. If Fatima had one wish, what would it be and why?

22. What is Fatima's roommate doing while this monologue is taking place?

23. What is your favorite line in the monologue and why?

24. When Fatima speaks as Raul, will you use a Spanish accent? Why or why not?

25. Find ten words in Fatima's monologue that you feel stand out as being the most descriptive of the overall purpose of the scene.

LAB SCENE #4

NICK, male, age 27

Nick is a young, wealthy bachelor who owns a string of hair salons. He would love to meet a woman to become his wife. In this monologue, he is at his brother Jack's wedding and meets up with his cousin, whom he has not seen in a long time. They are on the balcony just off the dance floor.

NICK: Remember when we went swimming that year before Pops had cleaned the pool? It was so cold and nasty, but we didn't care! We just wanted to get summer started, and somehow swimming was the key. The next day the sun came out and Pops cleaned the pool—it was a perfect pool day! But we were all stuck inside with colds, and I ended up getting an ear infection. *(Teasingly.)* You know, Pops told me not to tell you, but when he cleaned the pool, there were all sorts of creatures in it! I'm not kidding! *(Silence as a girl walks by.)* Whoa! Who's that? She's totally hot! She looks kind of like Kyle's wife—oh. She is. You know, that's been my luck. All through college, I would meet these pretty girls, and we would get along really well. We'd go out, and at the end of the night I'd be ready to make my move, and she'd say, "Nick, you're really sweet, but I'm just not ready for a relationship." Next thing I knew, they'd be dating one of my friends and calling me for advice! Like I'd know the difference between a relationship and a hole in the ground! *(Slumps into a chair.)* It's all my mom's fault. She always made sure I was nice... polite. The girls would hear me say "Yes, ma'am" to a teacher and they would all say, "Oh, that's so sweet!" But, Kyle, man, he was a real jerk! He never said more than two words in our geometry class. A pretty girl would walk in and the rest of us would just stare at her. Kyle would pretend not to notice—or maybe he really didn't. I don't know—but that girl would sit down right next to him. She'd act like she'd dropped her pencil, and he would ignore her. By the end of the first day, she was asking everyone who that cute, serious boy was. When he met Ginger, she totally snubbed him, and do you know what? He ate it up! He acted like she was the last girl on Earth, and she acted like she didn't want anything to do with him. *(Pause.)* Guess what? When he decided to ask her to marry him, who do you think he called for advice? Yup. Me. The old Relationship Guru himself—Nicky-I-Just-Want-To-Be-Friends. That's me. *(Stands.)* You want to hear something funny? I bought these hair salons, so I'm around women all the time, right? You'd think I could meet someone special? There's this one girl, Sasha, at one of the salons. I'm thinking of asking her out. But before I could get up the nerve, she says, "You're really nice, Nick. You got a good-looking friend you could set me up with?" *(Points.)* That's her—with Jack.

NAME ______________________________ PERIOD ______ DATE ____________

NICK

Answer the following questions about the character, Nick, from Lab Scene #4.

1. What do we know for certain about Nick?

2. What do we know for certain about the setting?

3. What year do you think it is? Why?

4. What is the scene about?

5. Is the scene comic, dramatic, or a combination of the two?

6. What happened just before the start of this scene?

7. What do you think might happen after the scene if the story continued?

8. If this scene was from a play, what do you think it would be called?

9. What does Nick want in this scene?

10. If Nick repeatedly made a gesture in this scene, what would it be and why?

11. What are Nick's hobbies?

12. What object do you associate with Nick and why?

13. What animal do you associate with Nick and why?

NAME ________________________________ PERIOD ________ DATE ______________

14. In real life, would you be Nick's friend? Why or why not?

15. How is Nick like you?

16. How is Nick different from you?

17. What is Nick's most positive trait?

18. What is his status in the world? Does he have money or power?

19. What does Nick want from life?

20. What does he fear and why?

21. Who does Nick admire and why?

22. What are/were Nick's parents like?

23. If he had one wish, what would it be and why?

24. What advice would you give Nick if you were his cousin?

LAB SCENE #5

PHARRAH, female

In this scene, Pharrah is talking to the women and the girls. It's casual. Because there is no context to the scene, imagine various situations in which a strong, educated woman might be telling this type of story. Create your own context for the monologue, and even try putting in into several different contexts to see what works best for you. (Pharrah is pronounced "Farah.")

PHARRAH: When I was 7, I wanted to be an architect. My favorite book was about a dinosaur whose best friend was a saber tooth tiger cub, and they explored prehistoric Earth together. My mom bought it for a quarter at a garage sale. It was brand new! She read it to me every night. I would be the dinosaur, and she would be the tiger. I got to where I knew it by heart, but I also learned to recognize the words. And then the pages started falling out, so she put them into a scrapbook for me so that we didn't have to throw it away. She never got tired of doing things for me. Soon the scrapbook was filled with National Geographic articles, fossils, and fun things we found on our adventures. Every pre-pubescent wannabe archeologist should have such committed cheerleaders! Then, when I was in 7th grade, I had Mrs. Tucker's home room. She was so old fashioned. One day she invited me to have lunch in her classroom, and that made me feel very special. She said I was her brightest student, even brighter than most of the boys. Did you hear me? Brighter than... most... of the boys? Can you believe it? She was trying to make me feel good, but that was the first time I realized that some people actually believed girls were less than boys or that they belonged in different categories. She asked what I wanted to be when I grew up, and I told her: an archeologist. She made a sound. *(Makes sound of disgust.)* No. That wasn't quite it. It was more like this. *(Makes exaggerated sound of disgust.)* Yes. That's it. *(Badly imitating a woman's voice.)* "Pharrah, you might think you want to be a scientist now, because you're young. But when you become interested in boys, you'll change your ways! Boys like girls who are ladylike. There's nothing ladylike about archeology." My mom had made me a turkey sandwich that day. The bread was kind of dry. I was glad. That dry bread was what stopped me from saying the first rude thing that came to mind. The aluminum foil in my fingers, pressed into my lap, tightened into a dense ball and was beginning to feel a bit dangerous. With a full mouth, I chewed and chewed and chewed, which gave me time to carefully plan out what I would say and to drop the foil to the floor rather than hurtling it. I'd never even had a detention before, and I was pretty sure pinging the teacher with a foil ball would be, I don't know, at least out of school suspension. Finally, I swallowed. I leaned down to pick up the foil I'd dropped and saw the trashcan clear across the room. I aimed, heard Mrs. Tucker gasp, and shot anyway. Two points! No, that was at least a three pointer! Mrs. Tucker gave me a look, but it was lunchtime, and the rules were relaxed. Plus, she liked to make a big deal out of her special lunches. I took a big swig of my milk. It was warm and not at all refreshing. I wanted to burp, but Mrs. Tucker wouldn't have tolerated that from a boy, even on special lunch day. And I'm pretty sure she wouldn't have thought it was "ladylike." I resisted the urge. I slowly pulled my heavy backpack onto my shoulder and looked at Mrs. Tucker and said, "Thank you for inviting me to lunch. It was very informative." That was NOT what I was thinking, but it was safe. And then I made my way between the desks and headed for the door. But just as I was about to walk out, I turned to her and said, "Mrs. Tucker. Ladylike is overrated. And I am smarter than the boys. I'm ranked first in my class—all 112 of us, including every boy." She smiled. It wasn't a friendly smile. That was the smile of someone who wished a rule had been broken but knew it hadn't. I waved goodbye and left. Just then that burp hit me, and it was out before I could stop it. Just loud enough to be heard but not so loud as to sound intentional. But just in case, I followed it with a just loud enough "excuses me" and headed to my next class. Ladylike is definitely overrated!

NAME ______________________________ PERIOD ________ DATE ______________

PHARRAH

Answer the following questions about the character, Pharrah, from Lab Scene #5.

1. What do we know for certain about Pharrah?
2. How old do you think Pharrah is?
3. What year do you think it is? Why?
4. What is the scene about?
5. Is the scene comic, dramatic, or a combination of the two?
6. What happened just before the start of this scene?
7. What do you think might happen after the scene if the story continued?
8. If this scene was from a play, what do you think it would be called?
9. What does Pharrah want in this scene?
10. If Pharrah repeatedly made a gesture in this scene, what would it be and why?
11. What are Pharrah's hobbies?
12. What object do you associate with Pharrah and why?
13. What animal do you associate with Pharrah and why?

NAME ______________________________ PERIOD ________ DATE ______________

14. In real life, would you be Pharrah's friend? Why or why not?

15. How is Pharrah like you?

16. How is Pharrah different from you?

17. What is Pharrah's most positive trait?

18. What is her status in the world? Does she have money or power?

19. What does Pharrah want from life?

20. What does she fear and why?

21. Who does Pharrah admire and why?

22. What are/were Pharrah's parents like?

23. If she had one wish, what would it be and why?

24. What advice would you give Pharrah if you were her cousin?

LAB SCENE #6

JASPER, male, 20 and **CANDY**, female, 20

Jasper is a fun-loving twenty-year-old college student. He makes good grades, but not good enough to get into law school—his original intention. His girlfriend, Candy, works very hard for her grades, which are not that much better than Jasper's. She has just finished taking an exam and is nervous about the outcome. She becomes frustrated when she finds Jasper playing video games with his friends instead of studying.

CANDY ENTERS JASPER'S dormitory TV room to find him playing video games with some of his buddies. She is carrying far too many books and hugs them close to her as if for comfort.

CANDY: Jasper. *(Louder this time.)* Jasper!

JASPER: Oh! Hi, baby! *(Back to the game.)* I didn't see you—man! Got me! Didn't see you come in... Woo hoo! Got ya back! How'd you do on your anatomy exam? D'ya ace it?

CANDY: I don't know. He hasn't posted the scores yet.

JASPER: *(Still playing.)* Well, how d'you think you did? *(CANDY shrugs.)* Huh, baby? I didn't hear ya. You think you passed, got a B, what?

CANDY: Come on, Jasper! Can't you put that stupid game down for a minute and talk to me instead of the TV screen? *(The rest of the guys take this as their cue to EXIT, allowing the two some privacy.)* Bye, Andy. See ya, Vince.

JASPER: *(Slightly overlapping CANDY.)* See ya, guys. *(Turns to CANDY.)* Okay. Talk to me. What happened?

CANDY: Nothing happened. I just took the test, that's all. Maxwell takes his time getting the grades up. It's like he's into this whole "torture" thing or something. He's such a jerk!

JASPER: I thought you liked Maxwell...

CANDY: No, you're right. I do. I'm just anxious, that's all. This anatomy class has been a lot tougher than I thought it would be, and I'm having to work my butt off just to get a B. I haven't gotten less than that yet, and I don't want this class to be the first.

JASPER: *(Pulls her toward him, almost paternally.)* Poor baby...

CANDY: *(Pulls away, a bit too angrily.)* Stop it, Jasper! Don't patronize me!

JASPER: Baby, I'm not—

CANDY: And stop calling me baby! I'm not a baby!

JASPER: I just wanted—

CANDY: You sit in here with your "boys" and play that stupid Night Fighter game—

JASPER: Night Raider.

CANDY: Whatever! You sit in here like a little kid while I'm out working my butt off to make decent grades, and you get in there and ace tests in classes I can't even spell! Then you sit there so smug and act like it was not a big deal! *(Starts wiping away tears.)* And here I am all worked up and crying and yelling at you!

JASPER: It's okay, ba— *(Stops abruptly, realizing what he was about to say.)*

CANDY: *(Calming down a little.)* No. It's not okay. This... *(Referring to her current state.)* ...is not okay. I look around me, and everyone is having fun. I'm not having fun. I'm having a nervous breakdown.

JASPER: Look. Maybe I can help you. I mean, you're right. Stuff comes a lot easier for me than some people. But look at you! You can sing and act and draw and paint. You're an artist. I can't even draw a stick figure...

CANDY: Jasper, I appreciate what you are doing, but that's not the point. The point is—I don't like college. I'm not even sure it's what I want to do anymore. Every time I'm having to miss a party to study or miss going out with you to go to the library, I think, "This wasn't what I got into this for. I want to paint."

JASPER: Maybe we could take a semester off to—

CANDY: I don't want you to do anything just because I'm losing it! This is my battle, not yours.

JASPER: Truth is, this isn't where I want to be anymore, either. I mean, my grades are okay, but they're not great. They're not good enough to get into law school, anyway.

CANDY: But that's all you ever wanted to—

JASPER: Not all I ever wanted. There's something else. *(He hesitates. CANDY gives him a look that says "go on.")* I'd like to be a teacher.

CANDY: A teacher. You? *(They both chuckle.)*

JASPER: Yeah. Me. A teacher. High school. Political science, maybe. Or geography. Maybe become a principal or something. What about you?

CANDY: What about me?

JASPER: I mean, if you leave here, what will you do?

CANDY: I don't know. For the first time in my life, I don't have a plan. Maybe I'll just paint. Who knows? Look. I'm really sorry.

JASPER: For what?

CANDY: For taking all this out on you. I guess I just got jealous that you can play games and have friends. I miss that.

JASPER: Hey! I have an idea. Let's stroll on over to Maxwell's office and see if the old guy is through with his torture of hardworking college students! I'll pin him down, and you can drip water on his forehead until he gives up the test scores!

CANDY: I have a better idea. Let's walk down to the Frosty Q and make ourselves sick on banana splits. Then we can come back here and play Night Fighter until our—

JASPER: Night Raider. The game's called Night Raider. If you're gonna—

CANDY: Whatever. You know, I think you get too stressed out over the little details. You need to loosen up, learn how to have fun! *(She pretend punches him on the arm. He returns the pretend punch. They start for the door. She reaches for her mammoth stack of books, and JASPER pulls her away with a stern look. He puts his arm around her and they start OUT.)* Thanks. *(Almost to the door, CANDY looks longingly at her books one last time, then back to JASPER, who pretends not to notice.)*

NAME ______________________________ PERIOD ________ DATE ____________

JASPER AND CANDY

Answer the following questions about the characters, Jasper and Candy, from Lab Scene #6.

JASPER

1. What do we know for certain about Jasper?

2. What does Jasper want in this scene?

3. If Jasper repeatedly made a gesture in this scene, what would it be and why?

4. What are his hobbies?

5. What object do you associate with Jasper and why?

6. What animal do you associate with Jasper and why?

7. In real life, would you be Jasper's friend? Why or why not?

8. How is Jasper different from you?

9. How is Jasper like you?

10. What is Jasper's most positive trait?

11. What is his status in the world? Does he have money or power?

12. What does Jasper want from life?

NAME ____ PERIOD ______ DATE ____________

13. What does he fear and why?

14. Who does Jasper admire and why?

15. What are Jasper's parents like?

16. If he had one wish, what would it be and why?

CANDY

1. What do we know for certain about Candy?

2. What does Candy want in this scene?

3. If Candy repeatedly made a gesture in this scene, what would it be and why?

4. What are her hobbies?

5. What object do you associate with Candy and why?

6. What animal do you associate with Candy and why?

7. In real life, would you be Candy's friend? Why or why not?

8. How is Candy different from you?

9. How is Candy like you?

10. What is Candy's most positive trait?

NAME ______________________________ PERIOD ______ DATE ____________

11. What is her status in the world? Does she have money or power?

12. What does Candy want from life?

13. What does she fear and why?

14. Who does Candy admire and why?

15. What are Candy's parents like?

16. If she had one wish, what would it be and why?

JASPER AND CANDY

17. What year do you think it is? Why?

18. What is the scene about?

19. What do we know for certain about the setting?

20. Is the scene comic, dramatic, or a combination of the two? Explain.

21. What happened just before the start of this scene?

22. What do you think might happen after the scene if the story continued?

23. If this scene was from a play, what do you think it would be called? Explain.

LAB SCENE #7

ALIX, male, 12 and **SAM**, male

Alix is a twelve-year-old boy and an only child. His father recently died in a car accident. His mother has gone into a deep depression, leaving Alix to get himself to school in the morning, cook his own meals, and take care of the housework. Sam is trying to help him cope with all the changes in his life.

SAM is sitting with his legs crossed on the table in the middle of the ingredients ALIX is using to cook.

SAM: So… so, so, so. Not talking to me today, huh? Whatsa matter? Cat got your tongue?

ALIX: *(Shoots him a sideways glance.)* Shh! Mom's not feeling good. You're going to wake her up. And get down from there! What's the matter with you?

SAM: What's the matter with me? Hah! That's funny. *(Mockingly.)* "Get down! What's the matter with you?" What! You think you're grown up or something? *(ALIX ignores him.)* Whatcha making? Looks good. Wish I could have some, but I can't. Tried that once. Biggest mess you ever saw! It was a grilled cheese sandwich— you remember—right after your dad died. Your Aunt Paula came over to take care of you and your mom, and she made you a grilled cheese but you didn't want it, so I ate it. It tasted good, felt good going down. Trouble was, since I don't have a stomach, it just landed on the floor. Plop! Chewed up grilled cheese goop all over your mom's rug.

ALIX: Shut up!

SAM: Your aunt didn't say anything, though. She just figured it was you, you know? Your dad dying like that, she didn't want to upset you.

ALIX: Sam, why are you here? I told you… I don't believe in ghosts, and you sure as heck aren't an angel! Why can't you just leave me alone? *(EXITS the room with a plate of food for his mom.)*

SAM: *(Yells into the other room.)* You want me to leave? Say the word and I'm gone.

ALIX: *(Returns with the food still in hand.)* Shh! I told you, Mom's not feeling good. If you wake her up, she'll just start crying again. Just be quiet. And yes, I want you to leave! *(EXITS again.)*

SAM: *(Not moving. Stage whisper.)* I keep telling you—you are the only one who can see me and hear me. I'll tell you why I'm here. Like I told you before, I'm here to help you. *(Silence.)* You act like you're not hurting and that you have to take care of everything. You think the second your dad left this place you had to become instantly mature? *(Like an announcer.)* "Super Alix—never cries, even when he hurts real bad! Able to defeat sadness with a plate of sloppy joes!" *(ALIX returns empty-handed.)* I thought she was sleeping.

ALIX: She is. I left it on her nightstand. She won't eat it. But if I don't leave something, she'll think I don't care.

SAM: You really think so? Alix… you really believe your mom would think you don't care? How long has it been? Two weeks? For two weeks you've been doing and doing and doing so that she can cry, cry, cry. When's it going to end? You going to let her cry herself to death?

ALIX: *(Goes to push SAM, but his hands go right through him.)* Man, I said shut up! Just go away! Get out of here! I'm sick of you. I'm sick of everyone telling me that it'll get better. What do you know? What do any of you know?

SAM: I know, Alix. I know. It sounds cliché, but we all die. Some of us live short lives, others live long lives, and in the end we all die. Life is the story and death is how it ends. Kind of.

ALIX: What do you mean, "Kind of"?

SAM: Take me, for instance. I'm dead, but my story isn't over. I am still waiting for the ending. Once my story ends, then I can rest. Finally!

ALIX: You act like you're looking forward to it.

SAM: I lived a good life. I was happy. I had a wife and a child and a good—

ALIX: Wait a minute! You're just a kid! How could you...

SAM: That's just how you see me. You needed someone to talk to, and so you made me a kid—so you would have someone to help get you through this.

ALIX: Sam. You know, my grandpa's name was Samuel Melvin McAlister.

SAM: *(Overlap.)* ...Melvin McAlister. Yes, I know, Alix.

ALIX: *(Long silence.)* So. So you came to help me get through this. I made you?

SAM: Not really. I was "made" a long time ago. You kind of "conjured me up"!

ALIX: What's next?

SAM: I don't know, Alix. You tell me. It's all right there. You just have to find the strength to deal with what you already know is the truth. *(Pause.)* You okay?

ALIX: Yeah. I'm fine. *(Disbelieving look from SAM.)* No, really. I'm going to be okay. I, uh... thanks, Sam.

SAM: All right. Well, if you don't mind, I think I'll take one of these outside where they won't make such a mess. *(Grabs a plate of sloppy joes and starts off.)*

ALIX: Sam. Wait. My dad. He didn't suffer, did he? I mean, when he died, he wasn't in a lot of pain?

SAM: No, son. It was quick. *(Noise from the back room.)* Sounds like your momma's stirring. Maybe she could use a napkin? You think? Well, go on...

ALIX: *(EXITS. From OFFSTAGE, as SAM pauses to make sure his job is done.)* Hi there, sleepy head. Made you a plate of sloppy joes! Here, let me help you sit up. Listen, I need some supplies for a project at school. After dinner, do you think... *(Trailing off and picking up SAM'S line.)* ...you can run me down to the mall?

SAM: He's a good boy, son. A good boy. Everything's going to be all right. *(EXITS.)*

NAME ______________________________ PERIOD ______ DATE ____________

ALIX AND SAM

Answer the following questions about the characters, Alix and Sam, from Lab Scene #7.

ALIX

1. What do we know for certain about Alix?

2. What does Alix want in this scene?

3. If Alix repeatedly made a gesture in this scene, what would it be and why?

4. What are his hobbies?

5. What object do you associate with Alix and why?

6. What animal do you associate with Alix and why?

7. In real life, would you be Alix's friend? Why or why not?

8. How is Alix different from you?

9. How is Alix like you?

10. What is Alix's most positive trait?

11. What is his status in the world? Does he have money or power?

12. What does Alix want from life?

NAME ______________________________ PERIOD ______ DATE __________

13. What does he fear and why?

14. Who does Alix admire and why?

15. What are/were Alix's parents like?

16. If he had one wish, what would it be and why?

SAM

1. What do we know for certain about Sam?

2. What does Sam want in this scene?

3. If Sam repeatedly made a gesture in this scene, what would it be and why?

4. What are his hobbies?

5. What object do you associate with Sam and why?

6. What animal do you associate with Sam and why?

7. If Sam or someone like him came to you, how do you think you would respond?

8. How is Sam different from you?

9. How is Sam like you?

10. What is Sam's most positive trait?

NAME ______________________ PERIOD ______ DATE __________

11. What is his status in the world? Does he have money or power?

12. What does Sam want long-term?

13. What does he fear and why?

14. Who does Sam admire and why?

15. What are/were Sam's parents like?

16. If he had one wish, what would it be and why?

ALIX AND SAM

17. What year do you think it is? Why?

18. What is the scene about?

19. What do we know for certain about the setting?

20. Is the scene comic, dramatic, or a combination of the two? Explain.

21. What happened just before the start of this scene?

22. What do you think might happen after the scene if the story continued?

23. If this scene was from a play, what do you think it would be called? Explain.

LAB SCENE #8

MIRA, female, 29 and **TAM**, female, 17

Tam is a seventeen-year-old girl who is struggling to make sense of her life. Despite a loving and supportive home, she is unhappy. She is depressed and has decided to run from her sadness.

Mira is twenty-nine, but she appears much older. Like Tam, her life in her teens seemed like a huge burden. She chose to drink and do drugs to get through each chaotic day. Although she is clean now, each day is still a challenge. When she meets Tam, Mira feels an instant motherliness toward her and hopes to guide her away from a path of trouble.

The scene opens at the bus station. Mira has just arrived and she is resting before she starts the long walk to town. Tam ENTERS LEFT, waiting for her departure. She is a runaway, but chances are no one has discovered that she is missing yet.

TAM: Can I sit here? *(MIRA nods without looking to see who is talking.)* Thanks. *(Puts her backpack down so that it is between the two women when she sits. Takes a seat cautiously, not wanting to stare at the haggard woman next to her. MIRA stares at TAM'S shoes.)* I know. They don't really match. But, you know, I figured I'd be doing a lot of walking, so I put these on. I have some better ones in the bag. *(Looks at MIRA'S shoes.)*

MIRA: Yeah. It's a real fashion show out here. If you're not careful, the fashion police'll give y'a ticket. *(To an imaginary person OFF RIGHT.)* Hey, lady! *(Stands.)* Hey! Is that your kid? You better keep an eye on 'em. He almost got on that bus. Or are you sending him to Memphis alone? *(Responding to some OFFSTAGE gesture.)* Yeah, same to you. *(Sits.)* Some people ought not to have babies. Her on the phone and her kid making like he's goin' to Graceland. *(Pause.)* Your shoes ar'lright. You won't get no ticket. I'as just yankin' your chain.

TAM: I knew that. Fashion police.

MIRA: *(MIRA looks up at her for the first time and becomes transfixed by an eerie familiarity. When TAM catches her staring, the older woman becomes a little embarrassed.)* Whatcher name, kid?

TAM: *(Suspicious.)* Why?

MIRA: Why? Well, I dunno. Maybe I'm gonna go narc to that cop. *(Points.)*

TAM: *(Nervous.)* Crap! Where? Where? What the... Forget you. I don't need this. *(Grabs her bag and begins to leave.)*

MIRA: Whoa! What's this? Hey, sit down. I'll leave you alone. Sorry. I didn't realize you were the sensitive type. I'as just making conversation. There ain't no cop, tennis shoe girl. *(TAM gives her a warning glance.)* Hey, you don't wanna give me your name. What else am I gonna call you? Tam? *(TAM is shocked.)* Don't be so surprised. It's on your keychain.

TAM: It's short for Tamika.

MIRA: Tam's good. I'm Mira. It's short for Miracle. No, really, it is. My parents didn't think they were ever gonna have kids, and then just when my dad's about to retire, pow! My mom is pregnant at forty-seven! So they named me Miracle. It was pretty cool until the boys at school started calling me Miracle Whip. Before long I was Mayonnaise Girl, and you can just imagine where that went! So I shortened it to Mira. I hate mayonnaise.

TAM: Tamika is just Tamika. No history. We moved a bunch, so each year when school started and the teacher would call roll for the first time, she'd say, "Tamika Lang," and then everyone would turn to look at me like they wanted to see who the freak with the messed up name was. The teacher would raise her eyebrow at me like she expected me to say something. When I turned ten, I started going by Tam, but then people would see my name, "Tam Lang," and they would say, "Are you Chinese?" *(MIRA finds this humorous and laughs a strange laugh. At first TAM is offended, then she begins to laugh. MIRA'S laughter turns to coughing.)* Are you okay? Here, let me get you a drink. *(She fishes into her pocket and pulls out a few loose bills and some change. It falls to the ground.)* Wait, wait. I'll get you a drink.

MIRA: No, really. I'm okay now. Save your money. Looks like you're gonna need it.

TAM: I don't mind. I mean, if you're sick or something, I'll get you a drink.

MIRA: No, honey. I ain't sick. *(Indicates the money that TAM is picking up.)* Is that all you got? *(TAM looks up, a little embarrassed but not really knowing what to say.)* You ain't gonna get too far on a burger's worth of change, not when the fashion police are hot on your heels. Where you headed? *(TAM shrugs, ignoring the question in a shy but polite way.)* You runnin' away?

TAM: Uh, yes, ma'am.

MIRA: Don't "yes, ma'am" me. I ain't that much older than you. I ain't thirty, you know. *(TAM is surprised.)* I know, I know. I'm not much to look at. I've had a rough life. I been on the streets since I was 'bout your age. What are ya? Sixteen?

TAM: *(Without missing a beat or looking up.)* Seventeen and a quarter.

MIRA: And a quarter, huh? Does that make you older than seventeen by a whole bunch? What grade're you in?

TAM: I'm not. I dropped out—unofficially—today. And I'm leaving. I'm going to Miami to work. Then I figure I'll join the Army or Navy or something and become an officer. I'm a really good leader. And you get to travel and stuff. And you don't have any nosey parents breathing down your neck all the time or teachers looking at you like you're an alien or something. Or maybe I'll start my own business—an art gallery—or a tour guide business. I'll probably have to start off waiting tables, though, till I get something saved up or turn eighteen.

MIRA: And I'm gonna win the lottery, wake up beautiful, and get my daughter back and—oh, yeah, I'll be able to take cough syrup without thinking I'm gonna...

TAM: You have a daughter? *(She looks around half expecting to see a child but knowing she's not there.)*

MIRA: Had. State took her. She'd be about twelve. I'm going home to find her. That's where I'm headed. *(Points OFF LEFT.)* See those lights? That's where she is, and I'm heading there as soon as my feet start working again. *(Talking to her feet.)* Right, feet?

TAM: Why? Why'd they take her?

MIRA: I wasn't fit. I'd been on the streets a long time. I was an addict and a drunk. Her daddy was in the pen, and I was homeless. I'd go from shelter to shelter, and one morning I just got up and left. I got about three blocks away when I realized I had forgotten her, but I needed a fix real bad, so I figured I'd get hooked up and then go back and get her. But afterward, I just kept walkin' the opposite direction of the shelter. I don't even remember how far I'd gone, but I started feeling really lonely. I kept seeing her waking up and me not there and her screaming for me. Then I imagined that they wouldn't take care of her or she'd wander out trying to find me. She was only two. I started running back toward the shelter and some cops saw me running. They told me to stop, but I honestly didn't hear them.

TAM: What happened? I mean, you don't have to tell me. I'm sorry, I'll stop...

MIRA: They chased me down. I had a lot of crap on me, you know? Plus, I was higher'n a kite. I told 'em I lost my kid, but they just used that as another reason to lock me up.

TAM: So they took her.

MIRA: Nah, kid. That was just once. I screwed up a couple more times before they took her. Enough for her to remember what a loser I'd become, I'm sure. You're not gonna get far on that *(Indicates TAM'S money.)*, and you might as well hear it from me—don't think you like me much anyhow. You might end up waiting tables for a while. But y'ain't joining no army and becoming no officer. An' don't think a kid is gonna make it big in Miami. You're just running. I don't know what from or who to, but it's a dead end.

TAM: No, I'm not like that, I'm gonna... You see, I figure I'll... Well, I know this family, you see *(Realizing how stupid she sounds.)*, and they live on this island where your fantasies come true. Okay. It's stupid, I know. It's funny—you're running to the town I'm running from. *(Indicates OFF LEFT.)* My dad's based there.

MIRA: What's the matter? He beat you?

TAM: No! No way! No, my dad's real cool. My mom's cool too. I mean, my whole family's pretty normal, I guess, except for me. I'm different. I've always been so sad, all my life. I can't ever remember being happy. I'm always tired, and nothing makes me excited anymore. The kids at school don't make fun of me or anything. They don't even know I'm there. You know, other than my name being on the attendance, I don't really exist at my school. At home I'm just so lonely. I'm right there in the middle of that big house with my mom, dad, and my sister, but I'm not like them. I just want to close my door and stay in my room. I want to be left alone. I didn't think it was supposed to hurt this much. Being alive.

MIRA: Honey, it's really simple. You're depressed. You just need to get help. You seen a doctor?

TAM: Look who's talking!

MIRA: I'm clean, have been for a year, but it ain't easy. I made myself real sick when I was using. I ain't never gonna be in good health again. But, sweetie, it ain't too late for—

TAM: I don't want to talk to those Army doctors about this. They'd tell my parents I was crazy or put me on all sorts of drugs—sorry—and I'd end up loonier than I am now. *(Silence.)* Listen, I've got to go. I—I need to sort some things out. *(She starts OUT RIGHT, and MIRA quietly looks down at her own shoes. TAM realizes that she's still running but she can stop before it's too late. She feels a bond with the woman who tried to help her, and now it's her turn to help.)* Well? You coming, Miracle Whip? *(MIRA looks up, confused.)* Come on. I haven't got all night. It's four miles back to town, and if I have my key *(Feels for a key in her pocket.)*—yes! No one will ever know I left. *(As they EXIT LEFT.)* You ever sleep in a bunk bed?

NAME ______________________________ PERIOD ______ DATE __________

MIRA AND TAM

Answer the following questions about the characters, Mira and Tam, from Lab Scene #8.

MIRA

1. What do we know for certain about Mira?

2. What does Mira want in this scene?

3. If Mira repeatedly made a gesture in this scene, what would it be and why?

4. What are her hobbies?

5. What object do you associate with Mira and why?

6. What animal do you associate with Mira and why?

7. In real life, would you be Mira's friend? Why or why not?

8. How is Mira different from you?

9. How is Mira like you?

10. What is Mira's most positive trait?

11. What is her status in the world? Does she have money or power?

12. What does Mira want from life?

NAME ______________________________ PERIOD ________ DATE ______________

13. What does she fear and why?

14. Who does Mira admire and why?

15. What are/were her parents like?

16. If she had one wish, what would it be and why?

TAM

1. What do we know for certain about Tam?

2. What does Tam want in this scene?

3. If Tam repeatedly made a gesture in this scene, what would it be and why?

4. What are her hobbies?

5. What object do you associate with Tam and why?

6. What animal do you associate with Tam and why?

7. In real life, would you be Tam's friend? Why or why not?

8. How is Tam different from you?

9. How is Tam like you?

10. What is Tam's most positive trait?

NAME ______________________________ PERIOD ______ DATE __________

11. What is her status in the world? Does she have money or power?

12. What does Tam want from life?

13. What does she fear and why?

14. Who does Tam admire and why?

15. What are her parents like?

16. If she had one wish, what would it be and why?

MIRA AND TAM

17. What year do you think it is? Why?

18. What is the scene about?

19. What do we know for certain about the setting?

20. Is the scene comic, dramatic, or a combination of the two? Explain.

21. What happened just before the start of this scene?

22. What do you think might happen after the scene if the story continued?

23. If this scene was from a play, what do you think it would be called? Explain.

LAB SCENE #9

TEACHER and **TAYLOR**, student

TEACHER: Taylor, you're up.

TAYLOR: *(Not expecting this; confused.)* What?

TEACHER: You're up. *(Silence.)* Your monologue? You're next.

TAYLOR: Now? Today? You mean, like, right now? *(TEACHER nods, not amused.)* Right now. Oh boy. *(Stands. Pause. Sits.)* You know, I am not feeling well. I almost didn't come to school today.

TEACHER: But you did.

TAYLOR: *(Distracted.)* I did? *(Realizes.)* Oh. Of course. I did. *(Coughs.)* But I shouldn't have. I'm sick.

TEACHER: Taylor, do you have your monologue?

TAYLOR: Do I have my monologue? Do I have my monologue! Of course I—this is the one from the script, right?

TEACHER: The script? Taylor. The script? Really? They're all from scripts.

TAYLOR: I knew that. I totally knew that. Uh, yeah, I've got it... here. *(Points to head.)* Memorized, right? These are memorized? I'm doing the one about the... the b— ...no, the fa—

TEACHER: The orphan, Taylor. You were doing the monologue about the orphan child. Here. *(Hands Taylor a script.)* Look familiar?

TAYLOR: *(Looks at it.)* Of course! Yes. *(Looks some more.)* Oh, yeah, the orphan child. Man, this is good. This is sad. This is what I'm doing. Oh, my, this is so sad. *(Starts crying.)* Oh, my god, this is awful! This is terrible. I can't do this! This poor, poor child!

TEACHER: Taylor, not that part. Turn the page. The yellow highlight. That's your monologue.

TAYLOR: *(Reading.)* Yeah, whew. This actually looks familiar.

TEACHER: Noted. Glad to know you've seen it before.

TAYLOR: *(Reading.)* Much better. Much, much better. Yep. This is good. More me. Oh, yes, this is funny. The kid's resilient! Wow. Love this. Whew!

TEACHER: And that's the one you memorized?

TAYLOR: Yeah. This is the one. But no. I did not memorize it.

TEACHER: What were you doing when you were supposed to be memorizing the script?

TAYLOR: When?

TEACHER: When everyone else in class was memorizing their monologues, what were you doing?

TAYLOR: Who?

TEACHER: Them. The class. Last week, when everyone was memorizing their two-minute monologue, what were you doing?

TAYLOR: *(Mouths silently, but clearly shocked.)* Two minutes! *(Aloud.)* Studying. Yes. I was studying. I think.

TEACHER: What?

TAYLOR: What what?

TEACHER: What were you studying?

TAYLOR: When?

TEACHER: Last week, Taylor. What were you studying all last week when everyone else was memorizing their monologue?

TAYLOR: *(Tries to be polite.)* Let me break it down for you. I'll be honest. I didn't memorize the script because I was busy with more important stuff. I mean, this is important. Just not to me.

TEACHER: My class isn't important to you.

TAYLOR: Is that a question?

TEACHER: I don't know, Taylor. Is it?

TAYLOR: I'm confused.

TEACHER: Yes, you are. Look, I know you don't want to be an actor. You want to be a doctor, right?

TAYLOR: Yes. Like my parents.

TEACHER: Don't think of it as an acting class. Think of it as a communication class. In this room, with my unimportant lessons, you will learn many important skills. Can you think of any?

TAYLOR: Memorization?

TEACHER: Yes. That's one. Any others?

TAYLOR: Time management?

TEACHER: Certainly. That's a great one too. Doctors must be able to do both of these. So let's say you are in medical school and you failed to memorize something because you were preoccupied with another "more important" class.

TAYLOR: I wouldn't do that. That's medical school. That's super important.

TEACHER: And if you can't do it here, in high school, then what makes you think you can do it later, in med school, when the workload is more challenging?

TAYLOR: Well, I—

TEACHER: Taylor, that wasn't a question, either. That was an opportunity for reflection.

TAYLOR: But it was a que—

TEACHER: No, Taylor. It wasn't. It may have sounded like a question, but a wise student, one who paid attention in theatre class, would recognize the subtext.

TAYLOR: Subtext?

TEACHER: Yes. The sentence did end in a question mark, but it was rhetorical. It was meant to challenge your thinking... to take you beyond the obvious to a higher level of thinking. Higher level thinking exercises your brain, making it stronger, making you, a future doctor, better prepared for dealing with challenges. And you know, Taylor, not every kid who sets out to be a doctor makes it all the way. I'm not saying you're that kid. You're extremely bright and capable! But what are you going to do if you change your mind or don't make it into med school?

TAYLOR: I've already thought about that. I've met a few of my parents' friends who started out in med school but changed their minds or...

TEACHER: ...or were encouraged to take different paths...

TAYLOR: Yes. Because they weren't responsible. *(Long pause for self-reflection.)* I'm really sorry. I'm sorry I didn't memorize the monologue. You have every right to be disappointed. And I had no right to say your class wasn't important. I'm sorry.

TEACHER: It takes a lot of character to apologize... even more to admit you're wrong, and even more to change and to come out on top. It shows a lot of resilience. You know what I mean?

TAYLOR: *(Looks at script.)* Yes.

TEACHER: Taylor, do you need this class to graduate?

TAYLOR: Yes. I need a fine arts credit.

TEACHER: And I am assuming you will eventually need letters of recommendation from your teachers for your college applications?

TAYLOR: Yes.

TEACHER: And would you like it if I wrote you a glowing letter?

TAYLOR: I wouldn't expect you to do—

TEACHER: I'm sorry, what was that? You were mumbling. But hey, don't worry. In theatre class, I can also help you improve your diction and other communication skills. Because, you know, your patients will want to understand every word. They'll want to know they can count on you. Take a seat, Taylor. Sahid, you're up.

TAYLOR: *(Sitting.)* Excuse me. Can I try again tomorrow?

TEACHER: Take the script home, and this time read it. Memorize the highlighted part and rehearse it. It won't be full credit, but I'll give you another chance to prove yourself. But honestly, Taylor, right now I wouldn't trust you to take my temperature. But this is the beginning of the semester. You've got time to convince me otherwise!

NAME ______________________________ PERIOD ______ DATE __________

TEACHER AND TAYLOR

Answer the following questions about the characters, Teacher and Taylor, from Lab Scene #9.

TAYLOR

1. What do we know for certain about Taylor?

2. What does Taylor want in this scene?

3. If Taylor repeatedly made a gesture in this scene, what would it be and why?

4. What are Taylor's hobbies?

5. What object do you associate with Taylor and why?

6. What animal do you associate with Taylor and why?

7. In real life, would you be Taylor's friend? Why or why not?

8. How is Taylor different from you?

9. How is Taylor like you?

10. What is Taylor's most positive trait?

11. What is Taylor's status in the world? Does Taylor have money or power?

NAME ______________________ PERIOD ________ DATE ____________

13. What does Taylor fear and why?

14. Who does Taylor admire and why?

15. What are Taylor's parents like?

16. If Taylor had one wish, what would it be and why?

TEACHER

1. What do we know for certain about Teacher?

2. What does Teacher want in this scene?

3. If Teacher repeatedly made a gesture in this scene, what would it be and why?

4. What are Teacher's hobbies?

5. What object do you associate with Teacher and why?

6. What animal do you associate with Teacher and why?

7. In real life, would you like this teacher? Why or why not?

8. How is Teacher different from you?

9. How is Teacher like you?

10. What is Teacher's most positive trait?

NAME ______________________________ PERIOD ______ DATE ____________

11. What is Teacher's status in the world? Does Teacher have money or power?

12. What does Teacher want from life?

13. What does Teacher fear and why?

14. Who does Teacher admire and why?

15. What are/were Teacher's parents like?

16. If Teacher had one wish, what would it be and why?

TEACHER AND TAYLOR

17. What year do you think it is? Why?

18. What is the scene about?

19. What do we know for certain about the setting?

20. Is the scene comic, dramatic, or a combination of the two? Explain.

21. What happened just before the start of this scene?

22. What do you think might happen after the scene if the story continued?

23. If this scene was from a play, what do you think it would be called? Explain.

CHAPTER THREE NOTES:

CHAPTER 4

ACTING

NAME ______________________________ PERIOD ______ DATE ____________

DAILY BELL WORK - ACTING

Answer each question as your teacher assigns it, using the space provided. Be sure to include the date.

1. Date: ________________

   What do you think is meant by playwright's intent? Why is it important to actors?

2. Date: ________________

   Why is it important to know the play before attempting to develop the character?

3. Date: ________________

   List ways to establish mood in a scene. How would this affect the acting?

4. Date: ________________

   Imagine listening to the radio in the 1930s. Because there was no picture, actors relied on their voices for 100 percent of their acting. How do you think this influenced their style?

NAME ____ PERIOD ______ DATE ____________

DAILY BELL WORK - ACTING

Answer each question as your teacher assigns it, using the space provided. Be sure to include the date.

5. Date: ________________

   Imagine attending a silent film in the 1920s. Aside from occasional flashes of text, the entire story was portrayed through pantomime and music. How do you think this influenced the actors' styles?

6. Date: ________________

   Many years ago, actors were encouraged to speak a certain, acceptable way. Accents were erased, and distinctive qualities considered to be harsh were toned down. Today, uniqueness is more marketable. Explain why you think this is.

7. Date: ________________

   Write a tongue twister using the first letter of your name.

8. Date: ________________

   List every step of brushing your teeth; include even the smallest detail. Explain why an actor might benefit from carefully observing this or any other activity.

NAME ______________________________ PERIOD ______ DATE ____________

DAILY BELL WORK - ACTING

Answer each question as your teacher assigns it, using the space provided. Be sure to include the date.

9. Date: ______________

   What habits might actors give characters to make them unique? List ten.

10. Date: ______________

    Explain why posture is important in developing a character.

11. Date: ______________

    Explain why actors should warm up their bodies, minds, and voices.

12. Date: ______________

    Some actors let excuses like, "I'm having a bad day," get in the way of good character development or a good rehearsal. Why don't directors accept this as an excuse?

NAME ______________________________ PERIOD ________ DATE ____________

DAILY BELL WORK - ACTING

Answer each question as your teacher assigns it, using the space provided. Be sure to include the date.

13. Date: ________________

    Can anyone be taught to act? Why or why not?

14. Date: ________________

    What do you think about the link between actors, appearances, and success?

15. Date: ________________

    ____

    ____

16. Date: ________________

    ____

    ____

ACTING

Many people who have never acted think that acting is reciting with emotion. That is a part of it, but think of it as only the tip of the iceberg. There is a great deal more to acting than the audience ever realizes—that is, if it is done well.

Imagine going to a performance where a young actor is playing an elderly man. At times he is hunched over like a very old man whose spine is crooked. But perhaps he forgets to maintain this posture, and sometimes the audience sees a twenty-five-year-old "acting" like an older man. Perhaps the elderly gentleman character is from France, but the actor is not confident in his dialect, so the character sounds as though he is from some undiscovered country between France and England, maybe with a bit of German influence. When an actor is untrained, his performance becomes noticeable to the audience. They are continually reminded that this is a play. However, when an actor is polished and comfortable in his own performance, the audience forgets they are at a play and they become involved in the characters' lives.

Besides voice and movement, actors must also be fully aware of the play and how it is arranged. They must know and understand the difference between plot and setting, comedy and drama, and so on. It is also important that each actor who wishes to pursue a career in either theatre or film knows how to audition and then what will be expected of them at performances. However, in this class, think of each graded performance as an audition and each day that your teacher gives you to prepare for that performance as a rehearsal.

As you approach your first graded performance, if you have not already done so, you will want to understand the terminology used by those in the acting business. Furthermore, you should practice what is known as actor's etiquette or manners. Did you know that actors have a code of conduct for rehearsals? Timing is another important issue, an art that varies depending on whether you are doing comedy or tragedy, classic or modern, Eastern or Western theatre. With practice, you should feel comfortable with different pacing and tempo techniques.

By the time you finish this chapter, you will also understand how to mark or "score" your script. This helps rehearsals run more smoothly and allows actors to record action, pausing, and even breathing. There is also a whole new vocabulary associated with the stage itself. What do you do if the director tells you to take three steps left? Does he mean his left or yours? He means yours, and you will learn more about that at the end of this section. You will also learn what the different areas of the stage are called and where to stand to await your entrances.

Volumes upon volumes have been written on acting, so this is a very concise lesson. However, if you approach this as your basis and continue to build on it with additional classes and experience, you will soon have a solid understanding of the art of acting.

THE ACTOR'S VOICE

One of your greatest tools as an actor is your voice. With it you will add texture to the story, giving it a time and a place. You will also convey emotion and understanding, and your character will have an age and a history. However, in order to do this, you must sharpen your speaking skills. The voice with which one is born is rarely the voice one will take to the stage.

An actor's primary responsibility is to be heard, because unless the audience can hear the lines being spoken, they are getting only half the story. When onstage, each actor must project his or their voice to the farthest row in the auditorium. Even stage whispers must be loud enough to be heard while still sounding like a whisper. Besides volume, actors speak very clearly by articulating all of the sounds in a word. They must also learn to pronounce difficult words so that they can be understood.

Some of the parts that make up the actors' vocal "tool" are as follows:

1. **Soft Palate**—the soft tissue on the roof of the mouth towards the back
2. **Hard Palate**—the hard, bony part on the roof of the mouth
3. **Bony Ridge**—the bumpy, bony area behind the teeth
4. **Teeth**

The lips and tongue work with these parts, creating space, touching, or forming shapes. When the diaphragm pushes the air from the lungs and through the larynx and the parts above, sounds are made. Sometimes these sounds are voiced, meaning the vocal cords produce a sound that is carried with the breath. Other times the sounds are unvoiced. To understand voiced and unvoiced, try this activity. Hold out the "s" sound for five seconds. Now, do the same thing with a "z" sound. Your articulators are in basically the same position, but the "s" is unvoiced and the "z" is voiced. Do the same thing with "th" as in thing and then "th" as in those. Which is voiced? If you said the "th" as in those, you are right. What other sounds are voiced and unvoiced? Complete the chart to the left.

Say the words below. Check the appropriate column if the underlined part of the word is *voiced* or *unvoiced.*

	voiced	unvoiced
mop		
play		
bear		
quit		
ape		
chat		
thing		
yes		
edge		
go		
shop		
zap		
back		
light		
toe		
fly		

Vocal quality is also important. Can you recall an actor whose voice is "annoying" to you? How about one whose voice is soothing? Both of these are due to the quality of the actors' voices. Quality can be many things, but in general, it is the "pleasantness" of one's voice. It might have an unusual pitch (how high or low one's voice is) or it may be nasal (sounds like the speaker has a stuffed up nose). If a voice lacks inflection (a variance in tone), it is said to be monotone. A long time ago, actors worked hard to have a voice that was considered pleasant and normal, whatever that meant. However, as actors started to be recognized for their unusual voices, quality became less important, and uniqueness became the trend.

Today, unusual voices and unique dialects have a place in the entertainment industry, especially in radio. Because the listener must rely solely on the sense of hearing, those who market products seek voice artists who will capture and maintain the audience's attention. Listen to commercials for the next few days. Take note of what you hear. Imitate the actors, and ask yourself, "Can I do that?" Bet you can!

What is imperative, though, is that actors learn to control their voices. When one has control, they can have many vocal styles, and that means more flexibility for roles. In order to have control, the actors should understand all of the aspects of their vocal tool. Try this activity: Exhale all of your breath and assume a bad posture. Without inhaling, recite the Pledge of Allegiance at a natural pace. Go on, try it. What happened? You started to run out of breath, so you tried to speed up. Then your voice became aspirate or breathy. Then you had to pause for a breath or risk passing out, right? Breathing control has often been considered the primary basis for a great voice. Consequently, breathing exercises are often the focus of many rehearsals and workshops. Experienced actors will spend years toning their diaphragm, the muscle that works the lungs, so that they can have a superior voice and so that their pauses sound naturally placed. Now, try the activity again, but this time, sit up and take a breath at the end of each sentence. Follow the breathing marks below that many actors use.

/ short breath (or pause)

// medium breath (or pause)

/// deep breath (or pause)

I pledge allegiance to the Flag of the United
States of America, //
And to the Republic for which it stands, /
One nation under God, /
Indivisible, with liberty and justice for all. /

Hopefully, you had an easier time because you improved your posture and used the breath marks. Good posture and breath control are key to sharpening your acting skills. We will focus more on breathing later in the section.

Besides clarity, quality, and breathing, actors need to be able to use their voices to portray believable characters. For example, if a character is from a different region of the country or from a different country, the accent or dialect will need to be different from the actor's. Furthermore, the actor's voice will need to reflect the emotion the character is trying to convey based on the way the character would act, not the way the actor would. The actor may do this by changing the expression—the way a character stylizes their reactions to the events onstage—or they may change the level of energy, which is the power behind the voice. Some characters are loud; others have less volume while remaining very intense. This is the ability to emphasize without adding volume.

The students above stretch their facial and mouth muscles with "Big Face, Little Face." Start by opening your mouth and eyes as wide as possible. Hold for five seconds. Now scrunch your entire face so that it is small. Hold for five seconds. Repeat this several times. Next, when you make your face "big," stick your tongue out as far as you can and stretch your arms and legs so that your body takes up the greatest possible space. Hold for ten seconds. Then scrunch up your face and body, taking up as little space as possible while still on your feet and hold for ten seconds. Repeat the last two steps several times.

An extension on this activity will get your articulators ready for any tongue twister. The first is "Big Boat, Little Boat," and it works the lips. Start by making the sound of a motorboat with your lips, but keep them a bit loose. Now, tighten up the lips to make a faster, higher-sounding vibration. Repeat several times. Now exercise the tongue by trying "Big Drum, Little Drum." Start by making a big, loose sounding drum roll with the tip of your tongue, then try to speed up the air flow to create a tighter, faster sound. Again, repeat several times.

NAME ______________________________ PERIOD ________ DATE ____________

UNDERSTANDING THE ACTOR'S VOICE

Answer the questions about the actor's voice. Be sure to spell the answers correctly. Then put the numbered letters from the answers in the corresponding spaces below to decipher the mystery quotation.

1. A sound that does not use the vocal cords is called ___(1) ___ ___ ___(2) ___ ___ ___ ___.

2. An actor must ___ ___ ___ ___ ___(3) ___ ___(4) to make sure their voice can be heard at the back of the auditorium.

3. If an actor is playing a character from a different area, they may have to use an ___ ___(5) ___ ___ ___(6) ___.

4. ___ ___ ___ ___(7) ___ ___ ___ ___ ___(8) control has often been considered the basis for a great voice.

5. ___ ___(9) ___ ___ ___(10) is how high or low one's voice is.

6. If a voice lacks inflection, it is said to be ___ ___ ___ ___(11) ___ ___ ___ ___.

7. When air is pushed out of the lungs and through the larynx, the ___ ___ ___ ___(12) work ___ ___ ___ ___ ___ ___ alongside the palates, the bony ridge, and the teeth to produce sound.

8. Even ___ ___ ___ ___ ___ ___(13) ___ ___ ___ ___ ___ ___ ___ must be loud enough to be heard while still sounding like whispers.

9. A voice is labeled ___ ___ ___ ___ ___(14) if it sounds like the actor's nose is pinched.

10. Alter the power behind your voice, also called vocal ___ ___ ___ ___ ___ ___(15), to make the character's voice unique from your own.

Fill in the corresponding code to discover what Pliny the Younger (61-113 AD) said about our topic.

___(4) ___(10) ___(3)   ___(14) ___(9) ___(2) ___(9) ___(6) ___(8)   ___(2) ___(11) ___(9) ___(5) ___(3)   ___(9) ___(12)   ___(4) ___(10) ___(7) ___(4)

___(13) ___(10) ___(9) ___(5) ___(10)   ___(12) ___(13) ___(7) ___(15) ___(12)   ___(4) ___(10) ___(3)   ___(12) ___(11) ___(1) ___(14).

NAME ______________________________ PERIOD ________ DATE ____________

ARTICULATION ACTIVITIES

Say each of the following articulation exercises several times. Listen to the way the letters sound. Take turns with your classmates so that you can hear each other. Sometimes we can learn best by listening to others.

1. Which witch watched which watch?
2. A big black bug bit a big black bear and made the big black bear bleed blue blood.
3. Unique New York
4. She sells sea shells by the sea shore.
5. Peter Piper picked a peck of pickled peppers; a peck of pickled peppers Peter Piper picked.
6. A cup of proper coffee in a copper coffee cup
7. Few free fruit flies fly from flames.
8. Lesser leather never weathered lesser wetter weather.
9. Rubber baby-buggy bumpers
10. Theopholus Thistle, the successful thistle sifter, successfully sifted some thistles.

Have you ever read Dr. Seuss's *ABC Book*? It is a short book of tongue twisting fun for speakers of any age. It makes terrific practice for the actor's voice and characterization.

Also try *Oh, the Places You'll Go!*, *The Cat in the Hat*, and many others.

TRY THESE FUN AND EFFECTIVE VARIATIONS:

- Say the tongue twisters with a mini-marshmallow on your tongue, but be careful not to choke!
- Try saying the tongue twisters while holding the tip of your tongue.
- Try putting the inflection in different places throughout the tongue twister to change the meaning.
- Try using a British or southern accent.
- How many times can you say each one in one breath?
- Practice doing a stage whisper using the tongue twisters.
- Can you say them using a musical scale? Start low and go up, then back down the scale on each one.
- Say each one backwards!

Now write tongue twisters of your own for each of the sounds D, H, X (or cks), and M. Remember, a tongue twister is easier to remember if it makes sense, even if it is silly sense. You can put the key sound anywhere in the word, but it will have more effect if it is at the beginning. Write your tongue twisters in your journals or on a clean sheet of paper.

BREATHING ACTIVITY

Breathing is involuntary. Unlike many of life's other necessities, one can only live without breath for a few short minutes. A single simple breath supplies the blood with oxygen, which is then carried to the various organs. Even the skin benefits! By breathing fully and properly, the body works better, the organs are healthier, and the actor can be heard!

When we think of breathing, we often think of someone taking a deep breath while raising their shoulders and then lowering their shoulders as they release the breath. This is incorrect. The shoulders are not involved in the act of proper breathing. Try the activity below, repeating each bullet three times or until the activity has been mastered. By incorporating this into your daily warm-ups, you will experience proper breathing and an increased amount of energy. You will strengthen your diaphragmatic breathing and will find yourself projecting with greater ease.

THE HOT AIR BALLOON

- Stand and face your partner with your hands loosely hanging to your sides and your shoulders back (not stiff, just in good posture). Your knees should be directly under your shoulders, and your chin should be parallel to the ground. This will be referred to again as "perfect posture." Both of you take a slow, natural breath in through your nose and let it out naturally and slowly through your mouth. Did your partner's shoulders move? Probably a tiny bit, because when the lungs fill, the expansion of the chest cavity will cause some slight movement. If they appeared to move too much, as though the shoulder muscles were involved, let your partner know and try again until you are both satisfied with the results.
- Now place one hand on your diaphragm (the muscle that pushes air out of the lungs). It is between the stomach and the rib cage. Press in slightly and repeat the natural breath. Not much should happen except that you should be able to feel a little tightening of the muscle.
- With your hand over your diaphragm, take a slow, deep breath through your nose while counting to ten. Hold for five seconds and release through your mouth over the same ten count. This time you should have really felt some tightening of the diaphragm muscle. Find some space away from your partner and the others. With your feet shoulders' width apart, drop the top part of your body over so that you are bent at the hips—not the waist. Your arms and head should hang with no muscle control, and your knees should be slightly bent. Imagine you are a hot air balloon: your legs are the sturdy basket and from the waist up is the empty balloon, sagging to the ground. Now repeat the slow breathing activity above minus the hand on the diaphragm and, as your lungs fill with air, your body starts filling, too. Like a hot air balloon, you will fill from the base (your waist) up to the tips of your fingers—all in ten seconds. You will then reverse the process while exhaling. Keep the body thoroughly involved in the activity. (For variation, try the balloon activity for longer and/or shorter periods of time.)
- Assume the "perfect posture" described above. Moving only your mouth (and the muscles around your mouth), say "he \ he \ ha \ ha \ ho \ ho \ huh." Each syllable gets its own small breath (note the breath mark: \), and the entire line should be done in about three seconds. It's a bit like the deep breathing women do when they take childbirth classes. The last syllable, "huh," gets a thrust (like a punch in the stomach would sound). Start very shallow and unvoiced. Continue to "breathe" the line, getting deeper each time until you are as loud as you can be without voicing the syllables. Now add a quiet voice (a stage whisper), then a louder voice, and so on, until you are as loud as you can be without yelling.

NAME ______________________________ PERIOD ________ DATE ____________

THE ACTOR'S BODY

Aside from their voice, the actor's other great tool is their body. Using their body and voice, the experienced actor can be anyone they want to be, any age, any situation. Combining information, emotion, and their own personal style, the actor interprets the character. They analyze the character's posture based on age, health, social status, job, situation, and more. By adding the physical characterization to the vocal, a unique and interesting character emerges. By doing it well, the character is also believable.

Imagine a coal miner in his forties. He has six children and has just found out the mine is shutting down and he will lose his job. He has mined for over twenty years, and his health is suffering. Now imagine a banker in his forties, well-off, two children, fast sports car, tennis player. Can you see how they would stand, walk, gesture, and carry out everyday tasks? What if these two were twins? They started life the same, yet took different paths. If one actor had the job of playing both characters (which is often the case in "twin" shows), can you imagine how he might approach the characterization?

Compare and contrast the two brothers.

Imagine you are watching the miner drink a cup of coffee in a diner. Describe his posture, his hands, his movement, and maybe even the way he shifts his head.

Posture: ______________________________

____

____

Hands: ______________________________

____

____

Walk: ______________________________

____

____

How might he react physically to a loud noise from outside the diner?

How might he react physically to the waitress dropping a tray of food?

Now describe the banker, who is having a cup of coffee down the street in an upscale hotel restaurant. How is he different from his miner brother?

Posture: ______________________________

____

____

Hands: ______________________________

____

____

Walk: ______________________________

____

____

How might he react physically to a loud noise from outside the restaurant?

How might he react physically to the waitress dropping a tray of food?

THE ACTOR'S BODY CONT.

There are three basic types of stage movement:

- *Blocking* is the act of planning and carrying out stage directions. In some cases, the playwright gives the actors directions in the script. In others, the actors and director plan the movement. Remember that the audience will be "distracted" by movement, so be careful not to upstage other actors. Also, keep blocking natural and motivated. In other words, if there is not evident reason to cross from one area to another, then the movement will look unnatural to the audience.
- *Gestures* are the hand movements actors use to communicate or support communication. For example, a mother might shake her finger at her child as a way of reinforcing her line, "I told you not to go into the woods!" The same mother may use a gesture to send a message without supporting it with any dialogue. How might she gesture to the child to go to his room without speaking? How might she tell him to be quiet using only a gesture?
- *Business* is the little things an actor does onstage to appear naturally "busy," such as a painter cleaning her supplies, covering her paintings, and washing the paint from her hands in a wash basin. Remember the last time you had a long conversation with someone? You likely listened while doing other things, such as completing your homework, drawing pictures, or looking at your phone.

List some gestures and business actors might use in a scene about children at a playground.

The above movements without the proper expression would be empty and hollow, lacking style. There are several different types of physical expression that actors can use to stylize their movements. They are:

- *Body language* — a type of non-verbal communication that includes posture, facial expressions, eye contact, and even gestures
- *Facial expressions* — non-verbal communication conveyed with the face
- *Posture* — the way one holds their body
- *Pace* — how fast or slow a character moves
- *Rhythm* — the beat to which a character moves (bouncy, strutting, slinky, with a limp, etc.)
- *Quirks and habits* — the little things characters do that make them unique and original (adjusting glasses, twirling hair, taking the steps two at a time, etc.)

WARMING UP

Like athletes, actors must warm up their bodies before they start rehearsing or performing. Like singers, they must warm up their voices. Many even warm up their minds. Most high school and middle school directors require students to participate in warm-ups, and many professional directors host them as well. However, in some theatres, it is up to the actor to conduct their own warm-up routine. The following suggested warm-up routine is just that—a suggestion. Your teacher may have their own ideas. After you try the activities, discuss them. Decide what will and will not work for your group. After you are warmed up, have fun with the games and activities on the following pages.

Before a physical rehearsal or show, the cast usually begins by warming up for about fifteen minutes, just as dancers, gymnasts, and athletes do. By stretching the muscles, the risk of injury is greatly reduced. Many shows require great strength and stamina, too, and the warm-up can help in both areas.

Breathing—With your feet shoulder's width apart, hands hanging loosely by your sides, back straight, and chin parallel to the ground, do the fourth step of *The Hot Air Balloon* exercise described on page 94, saying "he / he / ha / ha / ho / ho / huh." Continue to "breathe" the line, getting deeper each time until you are as loud as you can be without voicing the syllables. Now add a stage whisper, then a louder voice, and so on, until you are as loud as you can be without yelling.

Articulating—Choose any of the tongue twisters from the *Articulation Activities* and repeat each one three to five times. Focus on over-articulating—emphasizing the sounds in an exaggerated way. When you have rehearsed for a few days, you may start noticing areas of concern, such as dropping ending sounds (saying "goin'" for "going") or substituting sounds (saying "bin" instead of "been"). Make a list of problem areas and create an articulation warm-up that specifically addresses those needs.

Stretching—Start in a standing position. Imagine something you really want dangling in the air above your head. With your feet glued to the ground, reach for it. After thirty seconds or so, it falls on the floor in front of you. Repeat this to the sides, and behind. You may then sit straight-legged on the floor and try the same activity imagining that the thing is stuck to your shoe but you cannot bend your legs.

Thinking—Imagine your character as an animal. Which animal would you be? Why? What characteristics of this animal does your character display? Imagine how the animal would move, what their voice would sound like, how this animal would get along with others, etc. Discuss the animals as a class and take note of how others in the group see your character. For variations on this activity, imagine your character as a color, an ice cream flavor, a household item, etc. You may even want to make a folder for your script on which you can create a collage incorporating these ideas for your character.

Besides being believable and unique, every actor wants to be uninhibited. An inhibition is that which keeps us from doing something because we're concerned how others may perceive us. We may think we look silly and that others will judge us, or we may fear seeming too enthusiastic. There are an infinite number of activities actors can do to help get rid of their inhibitions and to help them move better onstage. Try each of the following activities. Then respond to the activity on the lines provided.

The Mirror—In groups of two, stand facing your partner. Decide who will be "A" and who will be "B." "A" will start by slowly moving as though looking into a mirror while "B" duplicates the movement as if the mirror. After about a minute, switch. You can also try these variations on the game:

- Have one person lead while the entire class mirrors them.
- Plan a non-verbal scene using the mirror game based on waking up, getting ready for a date, or some other mirror situation. Perform it for the class.

What did you think of this activity?

____

____

How might an actor benefit from this activity?

____

____

Were you embarrassed about trying the activity? Why or why not?

____

____

Charades—Each student will write down the titles of five different movies on five little pieces of paper and fold them. Divide into two teams and put your movie titles still folded in front of the other team. Students will take turns picking one and acting out the movie title for their team to guess in a minute or less. There are standard gestures for charades, such as holding up a finger for each word in the title and tapping one's forearm once for each syllable in the word. Tugging your ear means "sounds like," and tapping your nose means "that's right." No talking is allowed.

What did you learn about movement by playing this game?

____

____

How might an actor benefit from this activity?

____

____

Were you embarrassed about trying the activity? Why or why not?

____

____

Picture Frame—Each student will write down a line from a poem, a saying, or a song lyric on a piece of scratch paper. You may do more than one. Fold it once and place it in the center of the room. Break into groups of three, four, or five and draw from the papers. Your team will have one minute to pose into a picture that could have this saying, lyric, or poem line as its heading. Then freeze and wait for the teacher. They will unfreeze you one group at a time so that you can look at the other groups' pictures. Try these variations on the activity:

- Bring in headlines to work from instead.
- Take pictures of the groups and create a wall with the saying, lyric, or poem line as its heading.

Why do you think this activity would help an actor with movement?

____

____

Even though the groups were frozen, how did they display energy?

____

____

Slo-Mo—Each student will select a simple activity, such as teeth brushing or making a pizza, and pantomime it in slow motion. You will only have about a minute. For variations try:

- Do the same activity while the teacher calls "slo-mo" or "fast forward."
- Have others guess the activity.

What did you learn from this activity?

____

____

Energy Circle—This is not as much a movement game as it is an energy game. However, in order to have movement, there should be energy. The entire class will stand in a circle. Decide who will start. They will clap at the person to their right, who will try to clap left at the exact same time. The second person will then turn to their right and "pass" the clap to the next person, who will again try to clap to the left at the exact same time. Start slowly.

Except for the first and last people, everyone will clap once to the left and once to the right. The primary objective is to clap at the exact same time as the person passing it to you. Once this is mastered, the objective changes to increasing the speed while maintaining the rhythm. Keep going around and around the circle until the teacher stops you.

What would be a situation in which this activity would prove most useful?

____

____

Energy Blast—This is a variation on the Energy Circle. Still in a circle, one person will start by making a one-syllable sound (or word) accompanied by a supporting movement. It should, like its name says, almost be a blast of energy. The person to their right will copy them, then the person to their right will go, and so on. When it gets back to the person who started the movement, they will again do the same movement and sound, but then the person to the right will start a new one, which will then be passed around the circle. Again, this must be kept in rhythm and the energy should remain high. The game will stop once everyone has started a sound and movement. There are some fun variations to this game including:

- Use facial expressions and movement but no sound (while keeping the energy high)
- Experiment with "intensity" rather than volume
- Use phrases and sentences
- Try different approaches to the same word each time around the circle. For example, one person might say "no" and everyone comes up with different ways to interpret the word. The next person may say "why," and so on.

Were you reluctant to participate in this game? Why or why not?

____

____

How might a rehearsal benefit from this game?

____

____

Styles Tag—In an open space, divide into groups of six to ten. For safety reasons, don't try this with groups any bigger than ten or with more than one group at a time. One person is "it." They will begin a character trait while trying to tag the others at the pace and style of that trait. For example, a monkey would chase the others quickly, while an old man would chase them more slowly. The others must take on this same style while trying not to get tagged. If you get tagged, you are "it" and must come up with a new style. For example, let's say the student who is "it" is a zombie, so everyone else must be zombies until someone is tagged. The next student is tagged and is a young girl on her cell phone, so all others become young girls on cell phones. That students tags someone, who becomes Winnie the Pooh, so all must become Winnie the Pooh.

What are some character styles or characterizations your class explored that might be useful in scene work?

____

____

Mime Race—Each student will list five common objects on five separate pieces of scratch paper. Collect them and set them aside. Select two teams of five. Each team will line up on opposite sides of the classroom facing the teacher, who will be in the middle. The last four players on each team will face away from their first players and the teacher. The teacher will draw a card and show it to the first players on each team, who will tap their team's second player on the shoulder so they can turn around. The first player will then act the word out. When the second player thinks they have it, they will turn to the third player and act it out. When one of the teams completes the race, the fifth player will whisper the word to the teacher, and if they are all correct, they win. If not, they must keep going, starting with the player who got it wrong.

What made this game difficult?

____

____

NAME ______________________________ PERIOD ________ DATE ____________

BASIC PLAY TERMINOLOGY

Unscramble the words in parentheses using the context clues provided.

UNDERSTANDING THE PLAY AND ITS PARTS

A story acted out by actors on a stage is a ______________ (ylap) written by a ______________ (rywtphialg), also known as the author. Once the play is written, a ______________ (pliusebhr) edits and prints the play, and then markets it to the public. The finished play book is called a ______________ (tpcsri).

There are many different types of plays. A ______________ (daram) is a serious play, while a ______________ (cdyeom) is a funny one. A play with a sad ending is called a ______________ (agteydr). Some plays are funny and sad at the same time. They are called tragicomedies. A play that makes fun of something is called a ______________ (rafec), and a play that is overly dramatic is called a ______________ (raodmeaml). There are plays with more than one act called full length and short plays called one acts. There are many other types of plays as well.

Plays, like stories, have several parts. The ______________ (inenginbg) or the exposition, sets up the story. Often, this is where the ______________ (titnegs), or location of the play, is introduced. The story then builds to a ______________ (cximla). After this, there is falling action, also called the denouement (pronounced day-new-MAH), and then the end. Throughout the play, the storyline, or ______________ (oltp), is developed.

GETTING THE PART

Actors attend ______________ (unsiaitdo), or tryouts, to compete for parts. All auditions are different. Sometimes actors will perform several ______________ (ogumolenos) they have memorized. Other times, the audition is a ______________ (olcd) reading. That is where the director tells the actors to read parts from the script. The actor does not know in advance what parts they will read. If the director likes certain actors but needs to hear them read again, they will post ______________ ______________ (alcl bkcsa) and the actors will audition again. The director will then cast the play. There will be an actor for each role and maybe ______________ (eeriunstddus) in case an actor is unable to perform for some reason. Often, these actors will have walk-on roles unless they are needed to fill in for the leads.

MOCK AUDITION

Divide into four groups:

The Producers (one to three students and the teacher): They have the final say because it is their money producing the show.

The Directors (one to three students): They are the artistic minds involved in the show. They make the decisions, but if the producers do not agree, the producers can override the directors.

The Assistant Directors (one to three students): They assist the directors. In auditions, they are mainly administrative, taking notes, running errands, and calling the actors up to the stage. They offer their opinions when asked.

The Actors (the rest of the class): They will be the ones auditioning for the parts.

Your class may approach this activity seriously as though it is a real audition, or you may make it improvisational, each building your own character and creating situations. Either way, here are the steps to follow:

1. Have the directors and producers pick a play or scene. You will need multiple copies, enough so that each actor onstage will have one each time the scene is read. Ideally, the entire class should have one. You may want to use one of the lab scenes from Chapter 3 of this book.
2. Give the actors a couple of minutes to read over the scene while the producers, directors, and assistant directors have a short production meeting. They will discuss what they want out of each character.
3. Assemble your actors in a common area, and the production staff in another to start the auditions. Start by asking for volunteers. This is a good way to see who is enthusiastic. Have the students act out the scene in front of the class. Give every actor a chance to read once before anyone reads a second time.
4. Have another short production meeting. Discuss who fits certain roles and make a callback sheet to post on the door.
5. Conduct callbacks. By this time the students are more familiar with the script, and the characters should really be taking shape.
6. Have your final production meeting of the rehearsal process and cast your show. You may wish to cast understudies too. Make a cast list to put on the call board. Be sure to thank everyone who auditioned.

NAME ______________________________ PERIOD ________ DATE ____________

REHEARSAL TERMINOLOGY

Unscramble the words in parentheses using the context clues provided.

Once the play has been cast, ____________________ (slhararsee) begin. The first is generally the read through. The actors sit in a circle to read and discuss the script. From this point forward, each rehearsal will strive to get the cast closer to opening night. Many directors like to start their rehearsals with warm-ups to exercise the actors' minds, bodies, and voices.

Both at rehearsals and away (but mostly away), the actors work hard to memorize their __________ (silen) so that they can have a smooth performance. They also spend many weeks learning about their ____________________ (hrcatsaerc), the roles in which they are cast. Each strives to unlock the mystery of their character's posture, movement, and body language and to use their hands to ____________ (esrgute) naturally, as though the action was the character's and not the actor's. The actor will work to give their character a unique rhythm that aids in the progression of the scene. Eventually the play itself must develop a rhythm so that it stays energetic and entertaining. Some experienced actors feel very confident in their technique; however, even the best actors still take direction from the ____________ (rteoidcr), the artistic head of the production.

Sometimes the script has __________ ____________________ (gaset ctiedisrno) written in with the lines, but often the director and actors decide when and where to move. This planning of the movement is also called blocking. Actors must memorize their blocking as well as their lines. Each __________ (rmsak) their script with a kind of "actors' code" called scoring.

LET'S GET TECHNICAL

About a week or two before opening night, the director and technical director will add the _____________ (hilgts) and ____________ (udson) to the rehearsal. These are called technical rehearsals. By this time, the set should be finished and in place and the actors should be using most of the ____________ (sorpp) that they will need in the play, such as cups and glasses, food, hair brushes, and any other items their characters need to carry out the action of the play. The cast will continue to work with the technical crew (also called techies) throughout the remainder of the show. Several days before opening night, the costumer and makeup people will arrive for the ____________ (edsrs) rehearsal. Many actors' performances change drastically at this point because, as one actor put it, "Getting into costume and makeup is like putting on the character's skin. You begin to look like them and feel like you think your character would look and feel, and with the lights and sound and the set, it's easy to start believing you are there!"

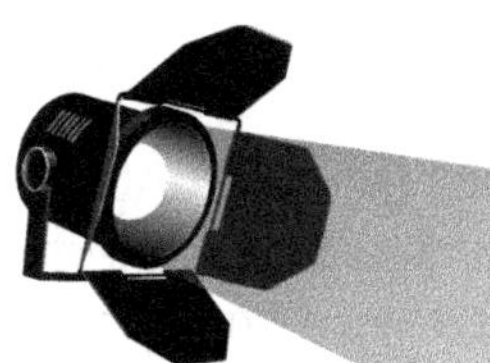

BASIC ACTING TERMINOLOGY

Now that you better understand the voice and the process by which your teacher will evaluate you, you need to familiarize yourself with acting. Acting is a lot like pretending, but at a much more sophisticated level. When we pretend, we use our imaginations to improvise another life. In acting, the playwright has written the story, so there is much less improvisation. The actor is a messenger; it is their job to communicate the playwright's message to the audience.

Most plays today are written in a representational style: they are meant to represent real life, naturally and somewhat realistically. The actors and the audience do not interact. Actors perform as though there is a fourth wall between the stage and the house, the part of the auditorium where the audience sits. However, throughout history and even today, some plays are written in a presentational style in which the actors break the fourth wall. Unless you've seen a melodrama, where this is always the style, you might be most familiar with this type of presentation from TV shows like *The Office*. In a way, the audience becomes a character in the scene, and the characters speak to them. These are just two types, and within each of these, there are numerous others, which will be discussed in other sections.

Regardless of the play style, as an actor you will need to find a way to portray the character in a way that fits the playwright's intent and also is entertaining to the audience. It is always wise to research a character before you audition for the part. If you are trying out for several parts within the same play, be sure to make each character distinct and original so that the director will see your versatility.

The process of characterization can be quite intimidating for student actors, but it does not have to be. Let's say you're auditioning for the role of Anne Frank's mother. There are several basic places to look for information about this character:

- What she says about herself
- What others say about her
- What the playwright says about her, both in the preface and in the stage directions
- What one can deduce from the subtext (what the lines imply but never say)

CHARACTERS ARE LIKE ONIONS

Imagine a yellow onion straight from the market. The "outer skin" is papery, brown, and dry. If you peel that off, you will expose the next layer, still brown and papery, but a little less dry than the first one. The next layer may be dry at the top and bottom, but white and moist in the middle. If you want to eat the onion, you will have to peel off several layers.

Characters are like onions: they have many layers and getting to the part that the audience wants to see takes working through each layer carefully. The first is in the text of the play—what is said about the character, what they say about themselves, and what the playwright may have said in the character description at the beginning. The next layers come from the subtext—what is implied in the text but never said. If the character is non-fictional, the next layer will come from what was said about the person throughout history or in the media. And the final layer comes from the actor's and director's own personal interpretations.

Peel a character today and discover the delicious and nutritious parts hidden beneath the outer layers!

If the character is historical like this one is, you can also do research online and in books. If the character is from a classical play that has withstood the test of time, read what scholars have written over the years. And then, of course, the actor will role score the character to fill in any remaining blanks and gain deeper insight.

Once you have discovered all you can about your character, you can decide if you want to play them emotionally or technically. Emotional acting, also called method acting, requires the actor to experience all of the emotions that the character is experiencing. Developed by Konstantin Stanislavski, a Russian actor and director, the actor is urged to become the character. One of his key conditions, the "magic if," encourages the actor to imagine how he would respond if he was in this character's situation, if he felt this character's emotions, if he had the character's relationships.

Technical acting allows the actor to explore the character from a less emotionally-involved perspective. Actors analyze the conditions (the weather, time period, time of day, etc.), the obstacles (what is keeping them from their goal), and the objectives (what they want from the scene or the play). They observe people who fit the character type and act out their observations, adding their own special touches. One downfall to technical acting is that actors are not as involved in their characters, and in the event that something unexpected happens during a performance, the technical actor will be less likely to respond as the character would than as the emotional actor.

As you grow as an actor, you will form your own opinions and preferences. Most actors use a combination of these styles, but a few are very loyal to a single approach. Always be open to trying out an idea before opposing it, allowing you to expand your skills as an actor.

Like any other group project, a group of actors must develop a philosophy of teamwork. Because they are together in such a small space for so long, many casts become like a family. However, once in character, there is a certain protocol for working with others onstage.

As an actor, remember to pay attention to the production schedule and always meet deadlines. Be punctual, and always remember to bring your script and a pencil—you will be making changes! It is a good idea to have a notepad, too, for taking down notes. Be off book (having your lines memorized) by the director's deadline, to establish trust and professionalism with your fellow cast members. Be quiet backstage before entrances and after exits. When the director calls "places," get there quickly and quietly, and when they call "cut," stop and quietly await instruction.

ACTORS' ETIQUETTE

1. Be on time to auditions, rehearsals, performances, and all other events.
2. Be prepared. Bring all materials and have them where you can easily get to them.
3. Meet all deadlines.
4. Be focused. Concentrate on the job at hand. Do not allow distractions to interfere.
5. Be brave. If the director asks you to try something new, don't shy away because you are embarrassed. However, NEVER feel that you have to do something that compromises your beliefs.
6. Be helpful. Find out what you can do to help others and offer assistance.
7. Be courteous. Never offer advice to the others. That is the director's job.
8. Be aware that you are one of several. Do not use rehearsal time to try new things or memorize lines without asking the director first.
9. Be your absolute best every time.

One group at a time, have everyone resume their positions so the other groups can discuss their picture.

Teamwork is also required onstage. In a play, when someone who should not have the audience's attention does something to steal it from the actor who should have their attention, this is called "scene stealing" or" upstaging." Instead, actors whose presence onstage is not the center of attention must master the art of staying involved in the scene without stealing it. Still, these actors should not be invisible. They must place themselves so that they can be seen by the audience. They shouldn't be blocked by scenery or other actors, and when a different actor crosses from one area to another, they must counter-cross to where they can still be seen. Moving naturally is the key—everything an actor does onstage must be motivated. In other words, there must be a valid reason within the play for the character to perform each and every action.

Besides being upstaged by scenery and other actors, you can upstage yourself by turning away from the audience. Because it feels more natural, actors tend to face whomever is speaking, even if doing so turns them away from those who are watching the performance. The term "cheating out" refers to when an actor compromises, facing a point between the other actor and the audience. But you still have to make it look as though you are addressing the other actor.

The director always has to consider stage dressing, placing actors to create a specific stage picture, so they will assign very specific places for actors. However, sometimes, especially during long monologues, the director will tell the actor delivering the monologue to "take the stage." This means that actor is free to move anywhere on the stage. Because of the unpredictability of this actor's movements, teamwork becomes especially important so that the stage picture stays pleasant and balanced.

FREEZE FRAME

Learning to create a nice "stage picture" in which everyone is sharing the space and no one is being upstaged is both an art and a skill. There are also a variety of styles, each appealing in the appropriate context. For example, directors generally try to avoid putting actors in straight lines onstage, preferring instead to stagger them about naturally. However, in a play in which severity of order is exaggerated, a series of straight lines may have an artistic appeal.

Gather a bunch of "lines" from poems, plays, advertisements, greeting cards, headlines, instructions, recipes, internet memes, and anything else you can find. In this exercise, creativity and variety are part of the fun. Cut them into lines, sentences, words, fragments, phrases, or paragraphs. Put them in a hat, and break into groups of five to ten. Each group will then draw a slip of paper from the hat and create a "photograph" using every member of the group. Remember that every person is important to the final picture. Use two minutes to create the picture and freeze while someone takes a picture so everyone can remember their position before relaxing.

ACTING TERMINOLOGY CROSSWORD PUZZLE CLUES

ACROSS

1. When the character has a valid reason for doing something, the action is __________.
3. Something that is implied but not spoken.
4. What the director says to get the actors ready to start the scene.
8. A play that has withstood the test of time.
11. What the director says to stop the action.
12. Something that keeps a character from their goal.
14. Each actor must develop a __________ character.
15. The process by which the actor seeks to make their role unique and entertaining.
17. An actor is __________ themself if they stand where the audience cannot see them.
18. During a long monologue, a director may tell an actor to __________ the stage, allowing them more freedom of movement.
19. A non-fictional character.
20. A play style that reflects real life.

DOWN

2. The style of acting that focuses on thinking more than feeling.
3. An actor is scene __________ or upstaging others if they distract the audience from the actor who should have their attention.
5. What the character wants from the scene or play.
6. The area behind the curtain where the actors cannot be seen.
7. To have one's lines memorized and not have to have the script in hand.
8. To move to another stage area.
9. The Russian actor/director who founded the Method style of acting.
10. A play style in which the actors address the audience.
13. To move because another actor has moved to block you.
15. When an actor compromises their body position so that the audience can see them, they are said to be __________ out.
16. Because the actors are so close for so long, they must develop a philosophy of __________.

NAME ______________________________ PERIOD ________ DATE ______________

ACTING TERMINOLOGY CROSSWORD PUZZLE

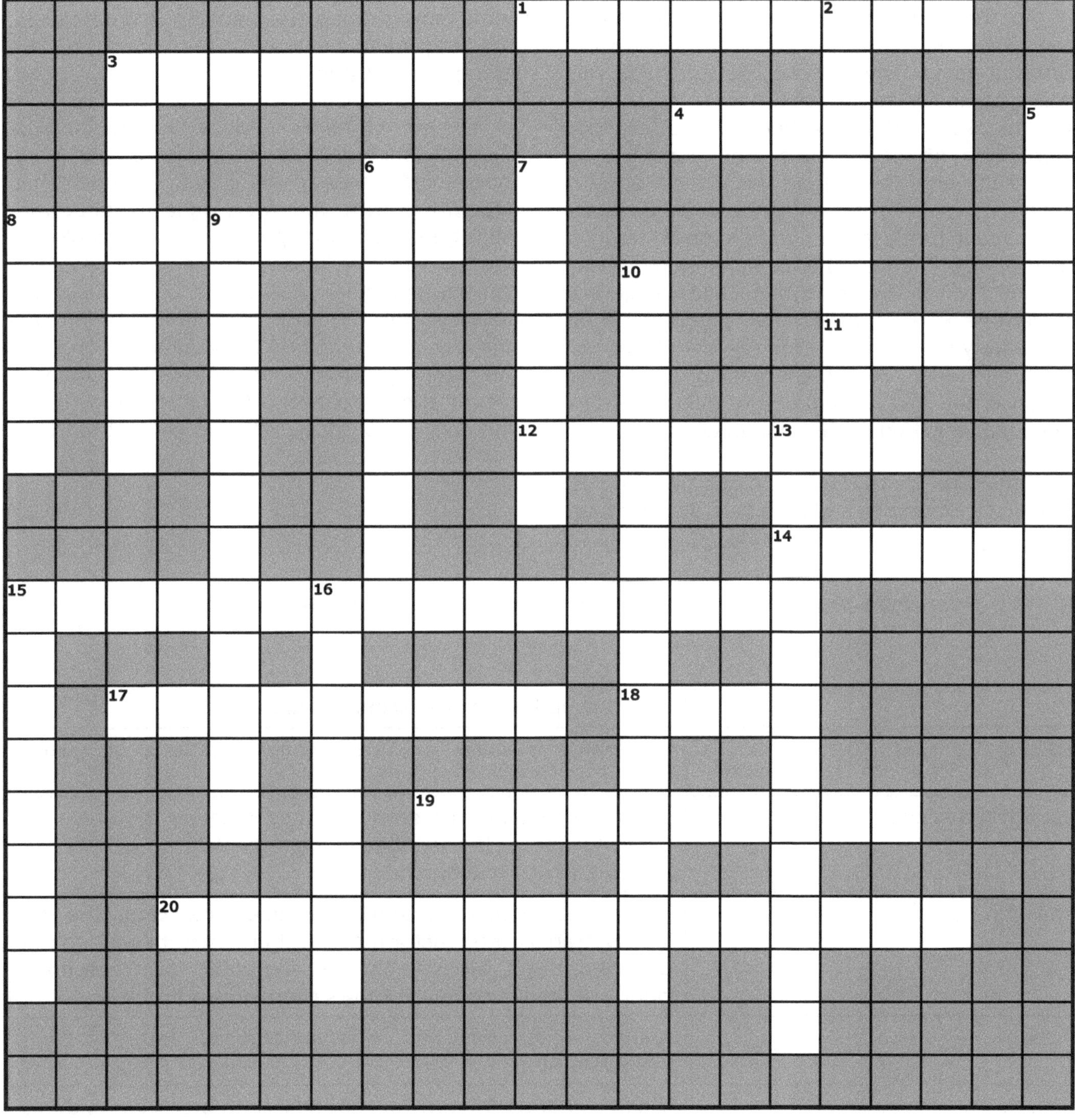

THE ART OF TIMING

Another important part of acting is timing, and different types of performances follow different rules. Think about the last time you heard someone tell a really funny joke. They set the joke up, then just before the punchline, there is a bit of a pause. The punchline is delivered, and then there is silence as the funny guy waits for his audience to laugh. Now, think about the last time you stumbled upon a soap opera. The timing is completely different, isn't it? Mysterious music that builds, lingering camera pans, long gazes, two people's hands that barely brush yet you can feel the electricity between them. Clearly, the pacing of building action in the joke-telling is very different from the building action of the soap opera.

Timing refers to the tempo and pace of line delivery, movement, and response. Actors must know how to keep their audience entertained, and they must be able to tell when they are falling short of this goal.

The art of timing cannot be taught. You must observe timing in real-life situations and bring those experiences to the stage. You must then experiment with what feels right, continue with what gets a good response from the audience, and learn from criticism. At the same time, you can use detective skills to get clues about line delivery from the script. The first step in doing this is to understand timing vocabulary and how the playwright uses punctuation in the script to convey their intentions. The terminology below and on the next page will help you get started.

ad-lib	To make up lines as the scene progresses.
beats	Sections of a scene. A scene is usually made up of several beats.
building a scene	The act of pacing the scene so that it keeps the audience eager for more. It has a beginning, a climax, an anti-climax (denouement), and an ending.
covering	The method actors use to hide mistakes in a scene. If a line is forgotten, another actor may say it or it might be fed to the one who forgot. Lines might even be made up. When done right, the audience never knows there was a problem.
cue	A line or other event on or offstage that tells actors to do or say something.
cut in	When a character interrupts another character's line with his own line.
cut-off lines	Lines that end abruptly without being completed. They are usually denoted with a dash after the last word.

dead space	Uncomfortable silence that is attributed to poor timing, weak memorization, or bad breathing. This is different from an intended pause.
fade-off lines	Lines that drift off without being completed. They are usually denoted with an ellipsis, which looks like three periods in a row.
holding for laughs	The process by which an actor pauses after a funny line while the laughter from the audience lessens; all actors remain in character.
overlap	The method by which lines or parts of lines are said simultaneously by different characters.
pace	The speed at which a scene progresses.
pause	A period of silence that is intentional and used to convey deeper meaning than lines are capable of doing.
picking up cues	Refers to actors and technicians doing their jobs without pauses that could pull the energy down.
tempo	The "rhythm" of a scene.
top	When one actor starts the next line immediately after the cue line; no gap is left between the two lines.

Imagine being in the following situations. Rank them from 1 to 5, starting with which you think would have the slowest timing and ending with which you think would have the fastest.

________ You woke up to realize you forgot to set your alarm clock. You have an exam in half an hour and you have to get ready.

________ You work at a fast food restaurant and it's a very hectic lunch time. You have a large order to fill but you stayed up late doing a science project and are exhausted.

________ You are in an elevator when your ex-best friend gets in. It's a long ride and you try to make polite conversation.

________ You are in your sister's room reading her diary to your best friend on the phone when you hear the front door. Within seconds the doorknob begins to turn.

________ You and your date just realized that you are running late for the movie, but you are having a great time just talking at dinner.

Discuss your rankings with the class.

NAME ______________________________ PERIOD ________ DATE ____________

CRAZY CLOCK

The Crazy Clock is confused. The timing terminology must go in the blanks, but where? Use the clues to figure out where each term fits. Have fun and good luck!

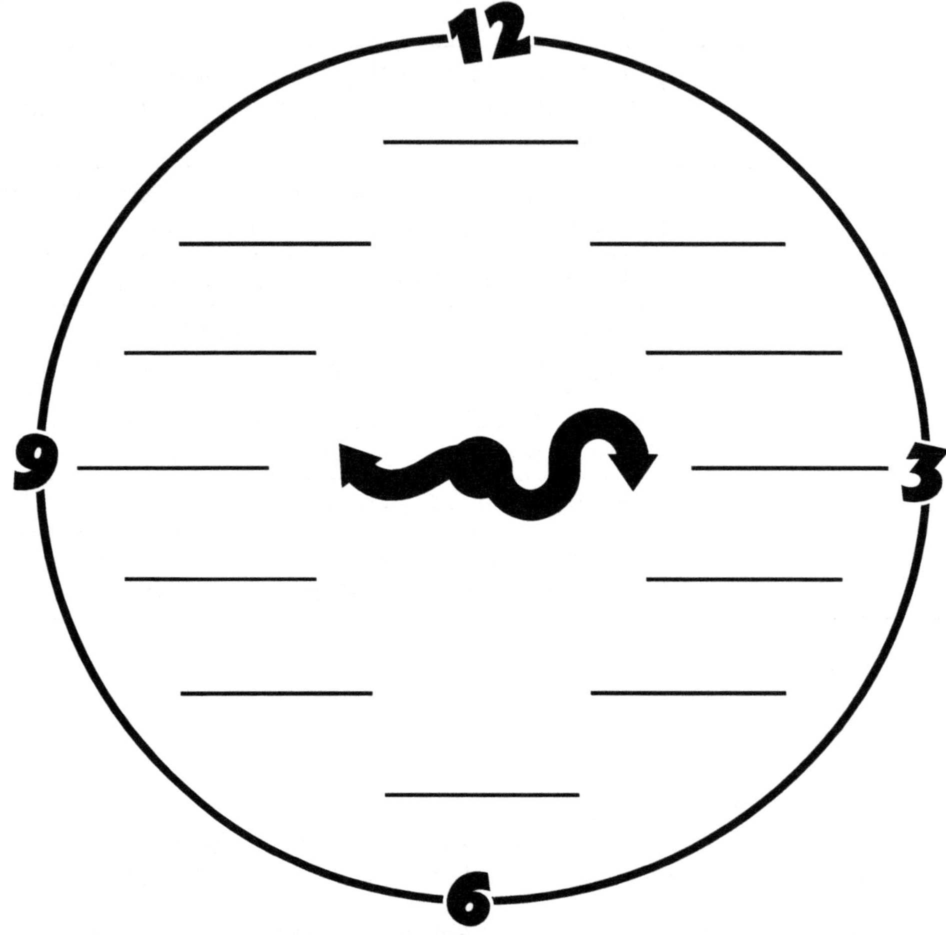

- "A period of silence which is used to convey deeper meaning than lines are capable of doing" is directly in the middle of *cue* and *ad-lib* in the evening.
- "The speed at which the scene progresses" is two hours before midnight.
- "When an actor says his lines immediately after the end of his cue line" is after noon but before *ad-lib*.
- "Pacing the scene so that it keeps the audience eager for more" is after *pace* and before *top*.
- "A line or other event on- or off-stage that tells actors to do or say something" is at lunchtime.
- "To make up lines" is at the South Pole.
- "Lines that drift off without being completed" is after *pace* but before *cue*.
- "Uncomfortable silence that is attributed to bad timing" is two hours before "the rhythm of a scene."
- "Sections of a scene that stand apart from others" is before *ad-lib* and after *cut-in*.
- "The method actors use to hide mistakes in a scene" is before *pause* and after *tempo*.
- "No space left between the two lines" is two hours before "sections of a scene that stand apart from others."
- "Rhythm" is three hours earlier than "speed."
- "Uncomfortable silence" is between *ad-lib* and *cut-in* but after "sections of a scene which stand apart from others."
- *Top* is five hours before "rhythm" and an hour after "making sure each scene has a beginning, a climax, and an end."
- "When a character interrupts another character" is directly across from *pause*.

NAME ______________________________ PERIOD ______ DATE __________

SCRIPT SCORING

For the first few weeks of rehearsal, most actors count on their scripts for lines, cues, and blocking. Many have their own, unique way of marking their scripts; due to the fast pace of the rehearsal, it may look like gibberish or chicken scratch to others, but the actor who wrote it will be able to read it.

It is a good idea to start by highlighting your lines in one color and stage directions in another. If you highlight your stage directions and the director has you do something different than what is in the script, draw a line through the highlighted movement and mark the new blocking in the outside margin. Next, choose a fine-tipped highlighter and begin marking character clues —anything the script or the characters in the play say about your character (including what they say about themself).

In rehearsal, always carry your script and pencil onstage until the director tells you not to. Even if it is in your back pocket, when you need it, it will be within reach. Other than the highlights, mark your script in pencil so that changes can be made quickly and neatly. Try to mark stage directions in the outside margin (away from the binding), because it is easier to see. The following is a suggested list of marks you may want to use when you mark your script.

X = CROSS	EN = ENTRANCE
D = DOWN	EX = EXIT
U = UP	/ = SHORT PAUSE
C = CENTER	// = MEDIUM PAUSE
R = RIGHT	/// = LONG PAUSE
L = LEFT	↑/↓ = STAND/SIT
↗ (wavy arrow up) = SPEED UP	___ = LIGHT STRESS (underlined once)
↘ (wavy arrow down) = SLOW DOWN	═══ = HEAVY STRESS (underlined twice)

Unless your teacher has asked you to follow a certain protocol, there is no wrong way to score your script as long as you can recreate the scene during the next rehearsal. Also, your understudy may need your script if they understudy for more than one actor. In that case, make sure you keep your markings simple and always create a key in the front or back of the script so that others can interpret your marks.

Use the above key to interpret the following stage directions:

1. EN DL X C: ______________________________
2. X UR ↓, read book: ______________________________
3. EX DR: ______________________________

Bonus: Using the diagram of a stage on the next page, can you figure out what shape the stage directions below are making? Can you make other shapes?

EN RC X UC X LC X DC EX RC

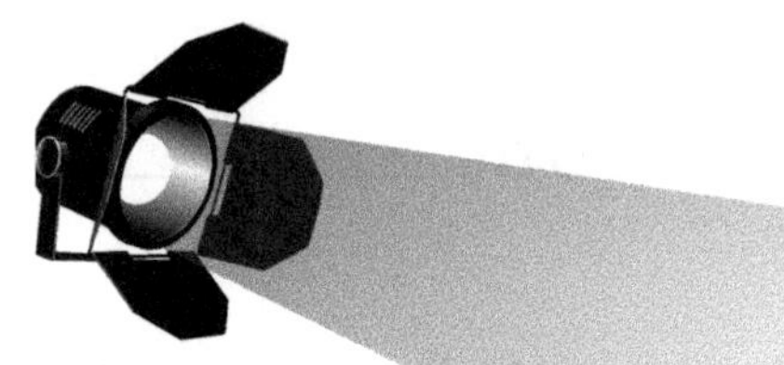

THE STAGE

UR	UC	UL
RC	C	LC
DR	DC	DL

AUDIENCE

- There are many different types of stages, but most high schools and middle schools have what is called a proscenium stage. A proscenium stage is usually rectangular with one side open to the audience; the other three sides are backstage.
- Small and medium-sized stages are divided into nine areas. Some medium-sized and most larger stages have fifteen areas.
- The area closest to the audience is downstage and the area farthest away from the audience is upstage.
- The terms right and left refer to the actors' right and left, not the audience's.
- The acting area is the part of the stage set aside for acting.
- When the actors are not onstage, they are backstage. This refers to the area behind the curtain or the set that the audience cannot see.
- The wings are the areas to the left and right of the stage where the actors stand while waiting for their entrances. The wings are also considered backstage.
- The building where the play is performed is the theatre or the auditorium.
- The part of the auditorium where the audience gathers is the house.
- The narrow area between the audience and the stage is called the pit. In a musical play, this is the area generally set aside for the orchestra. Many directors use the pit as an additional acting area.

ACTING REVIEW GAME BOARD

Use the 36 flash cards provided by your teacher to play the board game below. Up to four people can play. First cut the cards out and take a moment to study them. Then place them gray side down. You may use coins or other small objects for game pieces. Decide who will go first. Take the top card off the deck. Player One must define, answer, or complete the question. If they are correct, they may advance the number of spaces on the board game. If they are incorrect, they must go back the number of spaces on the flash card. Continue with Players Two, Three, and Four until one of the players reaches the end. Recycle used cards by placing them at the bottom of the deck. The first player to the end wins!

START Answer correctly to advance 3 spaces. →	Answer correctly to advance 2 spaces. →	Answer correctly to advance 3 spaces. ↓
Answer correctly to advance 2 spaces. ↓	Go to the space directly above this one before drawing your next card. ←	Answer correctly to advance 5 spaces. ←
Answer one question to move 3 spaces or answer two to move 6 spaces. If you answer two and miss either one, you must double the number of back spaces. →	Answer correctly to advance 2 spaces. →	Answer correctly to advance 2 spaces. ↓
Answer correctly to advance 1 space. ↓	Answer correctly to advance 4 spaces. ←	Go to the space directly above this one before drawing your next card. ←
Answer correctly to advance 2 spaces. →	Answer correctly to advance 2 spaces. →	Answer correctly to advance 3 spaces. ↓
Answer correctly to advance 1 space. ↓	Answer correctly to advance 2 spaces. ←	Answer one question to move 1 space or answer two to move 3 spaces. If you answer two and miss either one, you must double the number of back spaces. ←
Answer correctly to advance 2 spaces. →	Go to the space directly above this one before drawing your next card. →	**END**

CHAPTER FOUR NOTES:

CHAPTER 5
CHARACTERIZATION

NAME ______________________________ PERIOD ______ DATE ____________

DAILY BELL WORK - CHARACTERIZATION

Answer each question as your teacher assigns it, using the space provided. Be sure to include the date.

1. Date: ________________

   What are some ways you can research your character?

2. Date: ________________

   Tell about someone you have observed away from school. Using only their appearance, actions, and environment, explain the "scene" as though they were a character in a play. Be specific and creative.

3. Date: ________________

   What if your character from above met the character of the person sitting next to you? Read about each others' observed characters, and then describe the interaction between the two. Now add another neighbor's character and describe the scene.

4. Date: ________________

   Regarding the above bell work, how might your character change as more characters are added? Why?

NAME ______________________ PERIOD ______ DATE ____________

DAILY BELL WORK - CHARACTERIZATION

Answer each question as your teacher assigns it, using the space provided. Be sure to include the date.

5. Date: ______________

   How might one's character evolve as the environment or situation is altered?

6. Date: ______________

   What role does the character's goal play in the development of their onstage personality?

7. Date: ______________

   Why do you as an actor need to research your character? List the advantages.

8. Date: ______________

   Role score a famous cartoon character. Identify and explain their favorite color, food, style of music (or song), thing about themself. Also discuss their greatest fear, accomplishment, and ability. Finally, explain what got them to this point (the point at which a particular cartoon takes place) and where they will likely go after it is finished.

NAME ______________________________ PERIOD ______ DATE ____________

DAILY BELL WORK - CHARACTERIZATION

Answer each question as your teacher assigns it, using the space provided. Be sure to include the date.

9. Date: ______________

   Role score a famous movie character. Identify and explain their favorite color, food, style of music (or song), thing about themself. Also discuss their greatest fear, accomplishment, and ability. Finally, explain what got them to this point (the point at which the movie takes place) and where they will likely go after it is finished.

10. Date: ______________

    What might you as an actor discover about your character by researching the playwright? Why?

11. Date: ______________

    When a character is not clearly defined, why might the actor portraying the role need to know their favorite food, fears, or other unusual traits?

12. Date: ______________

    Define "stereotype" in your own words. List character stereotypes used repeatedly in TV shows, movies, plays, and other media. Why do you think we see these character portrayals used so often?

NAME ______________________________ PERIOD ______ DATE __________

DAILY BELL WORK - CHARACTERIZATION

Answer each question as your teacher assigns it, using the space provided. Be sure to include the date.

13. Date: ______________

____

____

14. Date: ______________

____

____

15. Date: ______________

____

____

16. Date: ______________

____

____

A WELL-DEFINED CHARACTER

We all enjoy cartoons. With larger-than-life color and energy and characters who defy the norm, cartoons depict life beyond our wildest imaginations. We choose programming that takes us away from day-to-day life. These shows allow us to imagine life on a deserted island or to see what life as the richest kid in the world would be like.

Complete the chart at the bottom of the page. Then imagine the characters you selected, but instead of being like you described there, they are average or normal. Would you still remember them? Would you be likely to tune in each week? Probably not. In fact, many TV shows make an attempt to imitate life, but rarely do those shows stick around for long. Most successful programs depict characters that exist in unusual settings with exaggerated characteristics, or they may have a plot that is way out of the ordinary. That is why they stand out so much amidst all the characters from the wide range of other shows.

Like the most successful shows, plays are usually riddled with unique characters. Each has an individual personality, personal habits or quirks, or a speech pattern unlike any other. They may emphasize words differently, walk with a particular gait, or use an uncommon facial expression. Actors work hard to preserve each character's individuality while making them believable. The result should be a cast of believable characters who are unlike the actors portraying them. Even those characters with few lines or little stage time should be clearly defined. Any actor who thinks their character is too small to be defined is cheating both themself and their audience of an entertaining and believable play experience.

As you are cast in various roles or as you practice scenes, you will want to study each character fully. Use the *Role Scoring* worksheet later in this chapter to fully flesh out your character. Find out all you can about what the playwright says about them. What does the character say about themself and what can be learned from what other characters say about them? Do the other characters tell any lies or make misleading statements about your character? Why? And what does that say about each of them? There is probably a great deal of information about the character in the subtext, that which is implied but not said in the script. For example, an actor may assume that a quiet person is shy. Learn as much as you can about the playwright to gain valuable insight into the characters. After all, one can only write what one knows. Finally, use your imagination to fill in any remaining gaps while remaining true to what you already know.

Think of three of your favorite characters from cartoons and children's shows, then describe them each.

Character	Show	What makes this character interesting? What are they like?

SAMPLE CHARACTER COMPARISON
using the characters from the cartoon *Scooby Doo*

CHARACTER	POSTURE/ WALK	APPEARANCE	HABITS/ QUIRKS	SPEECH	BEST QUALITIES
Shaggy	Hunched	Messy, baggy	Scared, hungry	Hippie	Friendly, funny
Scooby	Hunched	Dog collar	Scared, hungry	Rike a drog	Loyal, funny
Velma	Small steps	Frumpy, neat	Loses glasses	Intelligent	Smart, finds clues
Fred	Confident	Preppy, neat	Saves the day	Matter-of-fact	Handsome, brave
Daphne	Lady-like	Trendy, neat	Disappears or gets caught	Inquisitive	Pretty, kind

NAME ________________________________ PERIOD ______ DATE __________

YOU AS A CARTOON CHARACTER

Imagine yourself as a cartoon character. Choose a period of your life to serve as the cartoon. For example, a recent event may be memorable, or you might want to use last school year. It does not matter how long ago the event was, just that you have a good memory of it.

The following is a split character analysis similar to those you will be completing for your scenes in class. There are three columns. The first will give you a trait, and in the second you will analyze one of the cartoon characters you remember. Write the character's name in the box at the top of the middle column. In the third column, you will analyze yourself as though you were a character from a cartoon.

	CARTOON CHARACTER ____________	YOU
Describe the character's physical appearance including dress, hair, etc.		
How does the character talk?		
What are some of the character's most outstanding habits?		
Does the character work alone or with a companion? Describe.		
Does the character have a particular enemy or recurring problem? Describe.		
What is the character's best trait?		
What is the character's worst trait?		
What makes the character unique?		

NAME ______________________________ PERIOD ________ DATE ______________

ROLE SCORING

Answer the following questions in detail. Use any means available to find the answer. When you have exhausted all resources to find the answer, make one up. Explain any answer that you make up.

1. What play is your scene from?

2. Is it a monologue, duet, or a scene containing three or more characters?

3. What is the scene about?

4. What is your character's name? What are they like?

5. To whom is your character talking?

6. What happened just before the start of this scene?

7. What do you think will happen in the play after this scene?

8. When and where does the scene take place?

9. How old is your character? Are they mature or immature for their age? Explain.

CONTINUED ON NEXT PAGE

ROLE SCORING, CONT.

10. What do they do for a living?

11. What are their hobbies?

12. How does the title of the play relate to your character?

13. What does your character want in this scene?

14. If your character repeatedly made a gesture in this scene, what would it be and why?

15. What color do you associate with your character and why?

16. What object do you associate with your character and why?

17. What animal do you associate with your character and why?

18. In real life, would you be your character's friend? Why or why not?

CONTINUED ON NEXT PAGE

ROLE SCORING, CONT.

19. How is your character like you?

20. How is your character different from you?

21. What is your character's most positive trait?

22. What is your character's status in the world? Do they have money or power?

23. What does your character want from life?

24. What does your character fear and why?

25. Who does your character admire and why?

26. What are/were your character's parents like?

27. If your character had one wish, what would it be and why?

CHARACTERIZATION STUDY PROJECTS

Project 1: Character Mask

Using what you know about your character, design and make a mask. The mask should represent your character's fears, dreams, likes, dislikes, obstacles, beliefs, etc. It is only a representation; it is not meant to be worn. You will be graded on the following areas:

- Neatness
- Creativity
- Appeal
- Self-expression
- Half-page written explanation of how your mask represents your character

Project 2: Makeup Morgue

Create a one-page collection of pictures from magazines, newspapers, or other sources of what you think your character might look like or how they might be represented. If you were portraying this character in a play, this collection would be used to apply your makeup, so keep this in mind. You will want to consider age, status, gender, ethnicity, etc. Also, you may use just the individual features you think represent your character. For example, if you find a picture of a person whose eyes have the look you want but the rest of the face does not, cut out just the eyes. Be sure to include your name, the character's name, and the name of the play. You will be graded on the following areas:

- Neatness
- Thoroughness
- Creativity
- Following directions

Project 3: Costume Morgue

Create a one-page collection of pictures from magazines, newspapers, or other sources of what you think your character might dress like. You may also wish to use fabric swatches. If you were portraying this character in a play, this collection might be used to design your costumes, so keep this in mind. You will want to consider age, status, gender, ethnicity, etc. Be sure to include your name, the character's name, and the name of the play. If your character is from a different time period, you may need to make copies from books or research costumes online. You will be graded on the following areas:

- Neatness
- Thoroughness
- Creativity
- Following directions

CHAPTER FIVE NOTES:

CHAPTER 6

PUBLICITY AND OTHER PRODUCTION BUSINESS

NAME ______________________________ PERIOD ________ DATE ______________

DAILY BELL WORK - FINANCE AND PUBLICITY

Answer each question as your teacher assigns it, using the space provided. Be sure to include the date.

1. Date: ________________

   After purchasing scripts and paying royalties, you have $1000 left to produce a show. The actors are not paid. You will need to build a set, make a few costumes, purchase makeup, repair some lights, buy some music, and print posters, programs, and tickets. Create a budget for the show and explain how you will get the unbudgeted items.

2. Date: ________________

   What traits would you seek in the actor for a lead role if you were the director of an expensive play? Would it be different for an inexpensive show?

3. Date: ________________

   There has been a long-standing debate over the amount of money spent on athletics versus fine arts (band, drama, choir, speech, art, dance) in education. Explain your position on the subject as though you were a school board member.

4. Date: ________________

   Many directors host design competitions among the students at their schools to create the art for their posters. Others design their own, use what's provided by the publisher, or hire a professional. Which do you think is best and why?

NAME ______________________ PERIOD ________ DATE ____________

DAILY BELL WORK - FINANCE AND PUBLICITY

Answer each question as your teacher assigns it, using the space provided. Be sure to include the date.

5. Date: ________________

   Many schools with public address systems write "radio commercials" for upcoming plays. Some produce video commercials for in-house TV stations or YouTube. Write a "commercial" for a play at your school.

6. Date: ________________

   Do students at your school attend plays? Why or why not? What could be done to improve play attendance?

7. Date: ________________

   Should plays be performed as school assemblies? Explain.

8. Date: ________________

   Should the publicity reflect the mood of the show? Explain.

NAME ______________________ PERIOD ______ DATE ____________

DAILY BELL WORK - POSTERS, PROGRAMS, AND MORE

Answer each question as your teacher assigns it, using the space provided. Be sure to include the date.

1. Date: ______________

   What information do you think needs to appear on the poster? How might a school poster differ from a professional one and why?

2. Date: ______________

   Describe "audience etiquette" for a performing arts event.

3. Date: ______________

   What information do you think needs to appear in the program? How might a school program differ from a professional one and why?

4. Date: ______________

   Imagine you are in a play. The director has asked you to write a paragraph about yourself for the program. What would you say?

NAME ______________________________ PERIOD ________ DATE ____________

DAILY BELL WORK - POSTERS, PROGRAMS, AND MORE

Answer each question as your teacher assigns it, using the space provided. Be sure to include the date.

5. Date: ______________

   The program, poster, and other advertisements are generally created in the same color scheme as the costumes and set. Why is this important?

6. Date: ______________

   Create a time line for the poster, program, tickets, and other publicity for a show that has eight weeks of rehearsal. Remember to include time for design, approval, mailing, printing, and distribution.

7. Date: ______________

   ____

   ____

8. Date: ______________

   ____

   ____

PUBLICITY

Publicity is one of the most challenging jobs in theatre. Those helping with publicity for a show have to make sure that the public knows about the performance and that it sounds appealing. Of course, there is no exact formula for getting people to attend, since every school and community is unique.

In small communities where everyone knows everyone else, school-sponsored events may actually be the town's entertainment. Even if not involved with the school, friends and neighbors attend to support the young people involved. In large communities, however, the climate is completely different. Movie theatres and other venues compete with school shows for their audience. The best way to increase attendance is to plan well in advance and to publicize.

In planning your publicity for your show, consider the following:

Dates: Plan around other community events. Do not try to compete with popular sporting events, holidays, or professional theatre.

Price: Check with other entertainment venues in the area to see what they charge, not only for admission, but also for drinks and snacks. Price your tickets and concessions accordingly. If you have a large auditorium, consider giving complimentary tickets to local charities, community leaders, radio stations, newspapers, and your school faculty and administration to create a buzz and level of excitement in town. Besides, people who receive tickets usually bring another person who has to buy a ticket.

Show Selection: The single biggest determinant of your audience size is the cast size of your show, since most of your audience will be comprised of the family and friends of cast members. Choose a large cast show, or if doing a smaller cast show, how can you involve other students? Can you coordinate with the school art department to have an art exhibit in the lobby? Can a group of band or choir students provide pre-show and intermission entertainment? How else can you get more students involved the night of your production without being part of the production itself?

It's also important to choose a show that your community will want to see. Do not produce shows that have been seen recently at other area theatres or whose theme or topic go against the grain of the potential audience. For instance, if you live in a conservative area, *Laramie Project* or *Avenue Q* are not likely to be well-attended. Family-friendly shows don't have to be childish, and they will always bring you the largest audiences since entire families can come.

Form a Publicity Committee: Solicit help from the parent booster club, the drama club, other parents and students, and even other teachers. Can they promote it in their classes? Maybe offer extra credit to students who attend?

Publicize: Leave no stone unturned in your quest for free advertising. Your fellow classmates will make an excellent resource. Start early and get their advice on how to publicize your show.

What are some creative ways to publicize your show for free?

____

____

____

What are some things you can do to increase audience attendance?

____

____

LOCAL MEDIA

Of course you will publicize your upcoming show heavily on social media and your school and community's websites. But some people ignore all the advertisements they see online. That is why it is important to diversify your publicity to reach out to your community in a wide variety of ways. Consider these "old school" approaches in the chart below. They can still be very effective! Just make sure you leave yourself plenty of time as many of these will have deadlines several weeks in advance.

Name of Media	Contact	Phone Number	Email Address	Website
School Paper				
Local Paper				
School District Newsletter				
PTA Newsletter				
Local Radio Station				
Public Access TV				
Corporate Sponsors				
Other				

NAME ______________________________ PERIOD ________ DATE ______________

CREATIVE PUBLICITY

There are hundreds of ways to publicize in your community. Here are some creative ideas with space for notes plus space at the bottom to add your own ideas.

- Check with the elementary schools. Many send weekly packets home with the children. You may be able to reach a lot of parents and young audience members this way. Remember to use this method only when the show is appropriate for young audiences.

- Hang posters in places where people have time to read them. For example, rather than placing posters near store entrances and exits, ask permission to tape them to the counter at the checkout. The insides of restroom stall doors are also ideal (many businesses rent this space to advertisers). You might also try putting posters on the floor (use clear contact paper instead of tape), or on the ceiling at the dentist office. Remember, always ask permission.

- Ask the local restaurants if you can tape flyers to takeout orders or ask if you can stuff them in the bags at the market. Make bookmarks for the public and school libraries advertising your show. Where are some other places you can employ this type of advertising?

- Ask your friends and family to change the messages on their answering machines and voice mail to advertise the show.

- Offer to exchange ads with fellow schools or local theatres. You will advertise their show in your program, and they will run an ad for yours in their program.

- Other Ideas:

NEWS RELEASE FORM

Name of School: ______________________________

Name of Director(s): ______________________________

Title: ______________________________

Playwright: ______________________________

Presented By: ______________________________

Dates and Times: ______________________________

Location: ______________________________

Reserved Tickets? Y N Phone: ______________________________

Web Page: ____________________ Email: ____________________

Ticket Prices: Adult ________ Children ________ Students ________ Seniors ________

Synopsis or Description of Entertainment:

____

____

____

____

Event Sponsors:

____

____

____

Other Information:

PUBLICITY CHECKLIST

Name of Show: ______________________________ Dates: ______________

Publicity Chairperson: ______________________________________

Publicity Committee: ______________________________________

DUTY	ASSIGNED TO	DEADLINE	COMPLETED?
Announce cast on school PA			
Submit news releases to school papers			
Design program			
Acquire student biographies for program			
Get ads for program			
Print program			
Design poster			
Print posters			
Distribute posters			
Design and print tickets			
Design flier			
Print fliers			
Distribute fliers			
Invite newspapers to rehearsal			
Submit news releases to papers			
Submit news releases to radio			
Make school PA announcement			
Make picture collage for lobby Invite administration/board			

DESIGNING YOUR POSTER

Designing your show poster can be a great deal of fun, and the finished products make excellent souvenirs for the cast and crew. This worksheet will help you to design and print your show's poster and can also be used for project posters in class.

Decide on a budget for the posters:

$__________

POSTER CONTENT

Show:____

Playwright(s): ____

Presented by: ____

Dates: ____________________________ Times:____________

Location:____

Address:____

Ticket Prices: Adults ________ Children ________ Students ________ Seniors ________

*How will you credit the publisher *(see script)*:____

POSTER DESIGN

Who will design the posters?____

What size will they be?____

How many colors? Bleed or no bleed?____

When is the deadline for completing the design?____

COMPLETING THE PROJECT

How many posters will be printed?____

Who will print them?____

When is the deadline for getting them printed?____

When does the printer need the art to meet the deadline?____

Who will pick them up from the printer?____

*Crediting the publisher is a legal and contractual requirement in most cases and is generally specified on the copyright page of the script.

NAME ____ PERIOD ______ DATE ____________

Create a rough draft of your poster here. Use the space on the side to provide notes about colors, size, etc. Your finished product should be properly scaled and neatly finished.

DESIGNING YOUR PROGRAM

The best way to start designing your program is to have a few samples in hand. Many libraries keep programs from both local and Broadway shows in their archives. You may also be able to request these from your cast members who have recently attended shows. Keep in mind that there are professionals who will design your program for you should you choose.

Again, you will need to start with a budget. You may choose to keep your program simple or sell advertisements and make the program a great souvenir and moneymaker. If you have excellent parental support and assistance, you might choose the latter. However, if you find your group completing most tasks without assistance, you may be better off doing a simple, one-page program.

In general, the program should use the same art and same basic color scheme as the posters. Both posters and programs and any additional advertising materials should strive to convey the tone and mood of the show. For example, if your show is a lively, upbeat musical about love in the springtime, your posters, programs, and other publicity should reflect that with bright and lively colors and a whimsical design. On the other hand, a show about political oppression, lack of freedom, and lack of individual expression might employ the use of drab colors, shadowy figures, and a stark, jagged design.

The cover of your program should include your show's logo/title art (check with the publisher if you are required to use their copyrighted art, and if not, if you have permission to use it), who is presenting the program, and the dates, times, and location. Be original when designing your program, especially the cover. Try using a different fold so that the booklet is long and skinny or has an overlap. You may even choose to use a single, unfolded sheet of card stock for your program. This can be very elegant when the information is minimal.

The cast and crew are listed inside. The cast will be listed first with the character name to the left and the actor portraying the character to the right. These are generally listed in order of appearance and can usually be taken from the cast list in the script, which is usually listed the same way. Nonprofit and school shows generally list the crew under the cast in the following order: director, assistant director, stage manager, lights, sound, set, props, costumes, and makeup. Non-performance crew would be listed next, including publicity, ticket sales, house manager, ushers, etc. Like your posters, your program also needs to include the legal "Produced by special arrangement with…" statement that the show's publisher requires.

Some directors like to include a short synopsis of the play for their audience. You may also find it helpful to identify the locations and approximate dates or times of each scene. If your show is a musical, your audience will appreciate a list of musical numbers and who will perform them.

Other items you may wish to include in your program:

- A thank-you section for people and businesses who donated time, money, or supplies
- Pictures and bios of the students in the cast and crew, based on their completed *Biography Worksheet*
- Advertisements
- Pictures of rehearsals
- Advertisements for upcoming shows
- A reminder to turn off cell phones, not to take flash photography, and to tend to crying babies and children in the lobby
- A letter from the director or maybe the department head, principal, or superintendent
- An autograph page

BIOGRAPHY WORKSHEET

Complete this form and return it to ______________________________

by ____________________ for your bio in the program.

Name *(as you want it to appear in the program)*:

____

Character(s): ______________________________

Crew(s): ______________________________

Number of years in drama: __________ Drama club member: ☐ Yes ☐ No

Clubs and offices held: ______________________________

____

____

Other activities: ______________________________

____

____

Out of school activities: ______________________________

____

____

Previous roles in plays: ______________________________

Plans for the future: ______________________________

____

____

Special thanks *(remember those who lent you props, etc.)*:

____

____

____

____

DESIGNING FLIERS, TICKETS, AND MORE

FLIERS

Consider creating fliers that can either be sent home with students at all grade levels or distributed to area businesses. These can be designed using the same art as the poster and can even be miniature versions of the poster. However, because these will be mass produced, they should be printed as inexpensively as possible. You may want to have them printed two or four to a page, then cut them for distribution. Consider printing the backside in Spanish or another language common in your area. You may want to include a discount coupon so that people have a greater reason not to discard the flier.

Come up with creative ways to distribute the fliers (see the *Creative Publicity* worksheet earlier in this chapter for ideas). They should start circulating about one to two weeks prior to opening night.

TICKETS

There are two big decisions to make regarding tickets. First, will there be reserved seating or general admission? Then, will you handle ticket sales in-house or sign up with an online ticketing agency that works with schools? There are more and more of these companies every year, and you might find that the ease and convenience of letting someone else handle ticketing is worth the small fee, especially if your school will be doing multiple performances.

If you are not using an outside company, then you'll need to design the tickets, and, if using reserved seating, figure out if you're writing the seat assignment on each ticket by hand or getting them professionally printed. Either way, the tickets should include the show title, who is presenting the performance, the date and time of the performance that ticket is for, the price of the ticket, and if it's a special category, such as student, child, or senior. You might consider utilizing different colored tickets to distinguish between performances or categories. Two samples are below.

Try adding your own personal flare by cutting the tickets in an unusual shape rather than the typically shaped tickets below. For example, use a die-cutting device to make butterfly-shaped tickets for *Butterflies Are Free* or pine trees for *The Best Christmas Pageant Ever*.

Smallville High School presents
HAMLET
By William Shakespeare
April 30, 2020 • 7:30 pm

Smallville High School presents
HAMLET
By William Shakespeare
April 25, 26, 27, 28 • 7:30 pm

ADMIT ONE
6 - Student
General Admission

T-SHIRTS

Show t-shirts are like walking billboards advertising your upcoming production if you can get them a few weeks in advance and determine some days that everyone in the cast and crew will wear their shirts. They also make wonderful keepsakes after the show, especially if you print the production dates on the shirts.

Of course, the design on the shirts should tie in with the posters and program. You might be able to order shirts through the play publisher, and some even let you choose the color of your shirt and the color of your ink. Alternatively, if using the publisher's title art, you might be able to purchase a graphics package from them, then have the shirts printed at a local screen printer. Either way, it takes time to gather everyone's size preference, collect their money, and then actually get the shirts from the screen company. Start this process at least two months before opening night, especially if you want your shirts a few weeks in advance to help with advertising. And don't forget to consider parent volunteers, the school principal, and others who might appreciate a shirt!

VIDEO

It's fun to have your parents, the video production class at your school, or a professional company record your performance. However, first you have to find out from the publisher of the play if this is allowed. Some don't allow it, and the ones that do generally require an additional fee to be paid for the video rights. Even if you're not allowed to record the actual performance, you can still create a fun keepsake video that includes rehearsals, interviews with cast members, the makeup applications, and the cast party.

If you are allowed to record your entire performance, you can reach a broader audience by posting the video on your school's website or on a site such as YouTube. That way, even relatives who live far away can watch your production. Again, it is critically important that you first check with the publisher. Many don't allow this, and the ones that do will definitely require additional royalty fees.

PUBLICITY PROJECTS

Project 1: Poster

Select and read a play or use a play with which you are already familiar. Using the information from the plot, the playwright's notes, and your own interpretation, design a poster that communicates the mood and content of the play and publicizes a fictional performance. Your poster must contain all legal information required by the publisher, plus location and address, production dates, times, prices, etc. Write a brief description of your poster explaining all of your choices and attach it to the back of the poster along with your name.

Project 2: Program

Select and read a play or use a play with which you are already familiar. Using the information from the script, the playwright's notes, and your own interpretation, design a program. The program may be any size, and it must contain all legal information required by the publisher, the cast list, plus all pertinent dates, times, etc. Remember that the design, font, and colors should reflect the mood and content of the play. Write a brief description of your program explaining all of your choices and submit it with your completed program.

Project 3: Ticket and Flier

Select and read a play or use a play with which you are already familiar. Using the information from the script, the playwright's notes, and your own interpretation, design a ticket and a flier advertising the performance. Both may be any size and must contain all legal information required by the publisher, plus all other pertinent information. Remember that the design, font, and colors should reflect the mood and content of the play. Write a brief description of your ticket and flier explaining all of your choices and submit it with your completed project.

Project 4: News Releases

Following the format of the *News Release Form* earlier in this chapter, write three news releases for three real events at school. You will need to get the information from the most reliable sources. Events do not have to be theatre-related.

Project 5: Competitive Pricing

Find local printing costs for the following jobs for camera-ready art (no artist pricing needed). Format your findings in a creative but neat way. You must get at least three different price quotes for each item, preferably from the same companies. If you contact local companies, explain that you are doing research for a project and that your teacher may use the information you collect to purchase printing. You may also want to include online options in your research. Be sure to specify variations in paper weights.

Poster: 11″ x 17″, heavy white paper, full color; 100 pieces

Program: 8 1/2″ x 11″, one sheet white bond, full color, two-sided, folded; 500 pieces

Tickets: Eight-up on 8½ x 11″ white cover stock, one-sided, full color, trimmed out, crop marks provided; 800 pieces (100 sheets)

Fliers: One sheet white bond, two-sided, full color, tri-fold, 100 pieces

T-shirts: Twenty adult large shirts, brand name 50/50 no pocket T's, single color ink printed on front only

CHAPTER 7
PLAY PRODUCTION

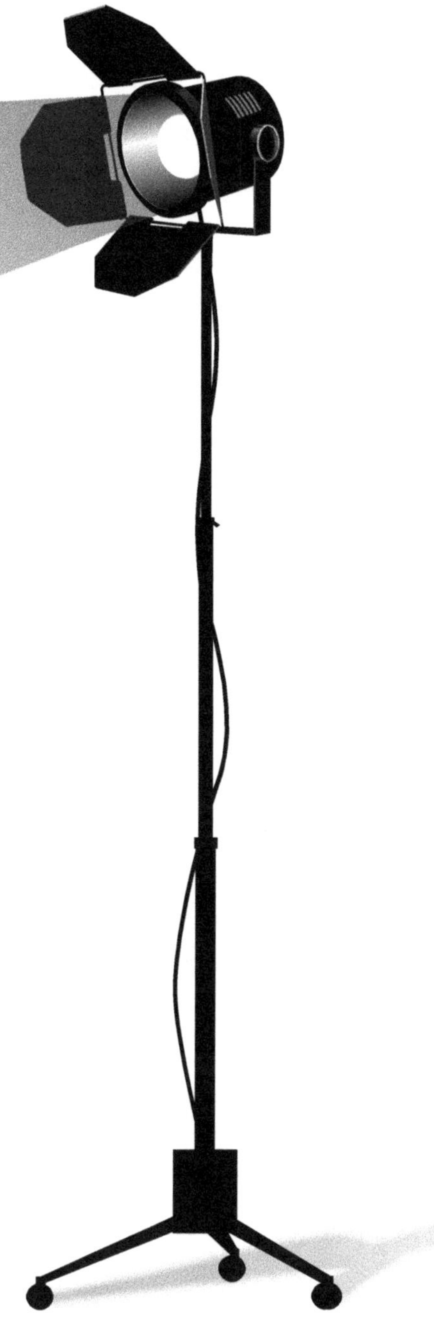

DAILY BELL WORK—PLAY PRODUCTION

WHAT MAKES A PRODUCTION?

The Production Staff

Creating Mood

Creating Mood Practice

Applying Stage Makeup

Finding, Making, and Buying Props

Costuming

Designing the Set

Lighting and Sound

PRODUCING PLAYS IN NON-TRADITIONAL SETTINGS

Virtual Theatre

NAME ______________________________ PERIOD ______ DATE ____________

DAILY BELL WORK - PLAY PRODUCTION

Answer each question as your teacher assigns it, using the space provided. Be sure to include the date.

1. Date: ________________

   Imagine you are doing a production of *Alice in Wonderland* for which there are many special effects. How might the director have Alice "fall through the rabbit hole" without interrupting the flow of the play?

2. Date: ________________

   Directors choose a color scheme for a play based on its mood. This is used in the set, the costumes, and the lighting and is often reflected in the posters and programs too. Why is color such an important part of a production? What effect might this have on the music chosen for the play?

3. Date: ________________

   Some actors do not give everything they have in rehearsal, claiming they are saving it for the show. How might this affect everyone else?

4. Date: ________________

   There are many jobs to be completed prior to opening night. In most schools, every student in the drama program is expected to pitch in. What kinds of tasks do you think need to be completed and which ones would you volunteer for?

NAME ______________________________ PERIOD ________ DATE ______________

DAILY BELL WORK - PLAY PRODUCTION

Answer each question as your teacher assigns it, using the space provided. Be sure to include the date.

5. Date: ________________

   Many actors get nervous before a performance. What are some ways this stage fright might be lessened?

6. Date: ________________

   Actors should generally avoid being seen by the audience in costume before the show. Why?

7. Date: ________________

   What are some realistic unexpected dilemmas that might take place on opening night? How can they be avoided?

8. Date: ________________

   What are some things parents could do to aid in the production process?

NAME ______________________________ PERIOD ______ DATE ____________

DAILY BELL WORK - PLAY PRODUCTION

Answer each question as your teacher assigns it, using the space provided. Be sure to include the date.

9. Date: ______________

   Many actors feel they reach their peak when there is a live audience. Why do you think this is?

10. Date: ______________

    After the final show, most directors strike the set immediately, even if there is a cast party. Why is it important for everyone to participate in the strike?

11. Date: ______________

    Many directors encourage students to mingle with the audience in costume after the show; others are strongly opposed to this. Explain which you would want and why.

12. Date: ______________

    Sometimes the items people lend to the show for props get broken or lost. What are some ways to prevent this, and how should the person be compensated?

NAME ______________________________ PERIOD ______ DATE ____________

DAILY BELL WORK - PLAY PRODUCTION

Answer each question as your teacher assigns it, using the space provided. Be sure to include the date.

13. Date: ____________

14. Date: ____________

15. Date: ____________

16. Date: ____________

WHAT MAKES A PRODUCTION?

When you attend a professional performance—a musical, for example—it is difficult to imagine everything that goes into making it a seamless, spectacular success. The actors are just one part of the production process, though we generally think of them when we hear the words "theatre professional" since they are the ones we see. There are numerous other people involved in a variety of jobs. Each individual performs specific tasks in different areas of the theatre, and only when it all comes together does a performance truly become a production.

At the top of the chain of command are the producers and the director. The producers are mainly concerned with the financial aspects of the show. They decide which shows will make the most money, and then they hire the best people for the job of making sure the money comes in and keeps coming in. Depending on the size of the show, there may be many different producers. In educational theatre, the producer is the theatre teacher's supervisor, principal, or other member of the administrative team responsible for budgets. Not only do they oversee the budget, they also often have final say on which show is produced.

The producers hire the director and sometimes the assistant directors. Because directors and their assistants work so closely together, many are hired as a package deal. The director is the artistic leader of the show and is most concerned with making the show work from an artistic point of view. However, sometimes "art" does not draw audiences, so the director and producers may have a "tug of war" over the final look of the show until they have reached a conclusion that satisfies both of them. In educational theatre, the director is almost always the theatre teacher and/or the choir director for musicals.

The technical director is in charge of the lights, sound, set, props, and maybe even the makeup and costumes. This person hires or assigns a crew chief to each of these areas, and they, in turn, hire teams to work with them. The show's director gives ideas to the technical director, who then creates plans on paper or using models, presents them to the director, and then makes changes to suit the overall goals of the production. Then the teams finalize the technical work, with the technical director making sure that deadlines are met and that the jobs are done to the director's satisfaction. Technical work can be very difficult, especially in settings such as public schools where actors and the tech teams share space. Often the set is built on weekends or late evenings so that rehearsals are not interrupted.

In educational theatre, the technical director is usually a teacher or a properly skilled parent. If your school is lucky enough to have a technical theatre teacher, they will likely serve as tech director on all plays. Many schools have active shop programs, full of students who enjoy the technical aspect of productions. This is great training to become a roadie for musicians, who need the same basic skills.

The stage manager is in charge of the backstage area during both rehearsals and performances. This person coordinates all of the jobs and serves as an information center. Using headsets, they receive cues and relay them to the crews, solve problems as they arise, and ensure that everything runs smoothly behind the curtain. The stage manager is often the one person who knows every aspect of the performance. For that reason, in educational theatre, it is usually a very responsible student or parent. If your program has two theatre teachers, one will often fill in as both tech director and stage manager, since the two jobs are closely related and one is mainly before the production while the other is only during the production.

The house manager ensures that audience members are comfortable and have their needs met from the moment they arrive for a performance. The "house" includes where the audience enters, where they purchase tickets, buy concessions, use the restroom, and sit to see the show, and the house manager is in charge of all these areas. This means they're also responsible for post-performance cleanup. In educational theatre, this is generally a job best performed by a teacher who has access to the school's Wi-Fi, general hallway lighting, supplies, keys, and so on. Plus, because concessions and/or ticket sales involves money being handled, schools sometimes require teacher oversight anyway.

When you attend a performance and are unaware of any shortcomings, it is because all members of the production staff worked together to make the show a success.

CREATING MOOD

The director reads the play carefully many times before auditions in order to have an idea as to how each role should look and sound. Once the cast is selected and rehearsals begin, the director's mental images solidify as the play comes to life. The performance should also convey a certain mood to the audience. The actors will do their part to create mood with their acting styles and characterizations, but it will also need to be evident in the lighting, sound, costumes, props, set, and even publicity.

Imagine a traditional play based on the story of Count Dracula. Now imagine Dracula's costume. It is probably mostly black with a cape. Now imagine his home. You are probably seeing images of a dark, dank castle with gray walls, dark corners, and grotesquely ornate furniture.

Color is one of the most obvious ways to create mood. Long before psychologists began studying color, society had already begun assigning meanings. For example, white became symbolic of purity, while red was associated with debauchery. Purple became the color of royalty, and brown was symbolic of simplicity. From a theatrical point of view, it is important to establish a color scheme for a play early in the production process so that it can be implemented throughout. A scheme is a selection of several colors that can be used throughout a play to support the message without overpowering it.

Another way to create mood is to manipulate visual lines. Soft, rounded lines come across as lighthearted, while jagged, edgy lines are perceived as harsh. Repetitive patterns are comfortable, but random, busy patterns are considered chaotic. A set designer can draw the audience's attention to a central place in a room simply by having all lines converge on that spot. Having doorways lean to the side and creating larger-than-life props can signal to the audience that a scene takes place in a dream.

Lighting and sound allow modern technology to play a role in the creation of mood, as does the introduction of special effects, such as fog and smoke machines. Lights can be colored with special sheets of thin plastic called gels. Gels come in thousands of colors, and, combined with special sheets of texture, they wash the set in moonlight, create the appearance of a crackling fire, or create a beautiful sunset. Imagine that sunset. What else does it need? How about the sound of crickets in the distance or a howling coyote, or maybe the sound of a twig snapping under a heavy boot? Add the sound and flash of gunfire, and suddenly the audience is in the middle of an Old West gunfight.

The idea of color and line creating mood can also be used in the selection of costumes and props, in the design and application of stage makeup, and in the publicity. Although color and line will effectively create the tone the director wants, it will lack dimension without texture to further support the director's vision. A polished, glossy finish such as glass, high-gloss paints, or

CONTINUED ON PAGE 156

NAME ______________________ PERIOD ______ DATE ____________

THE PRODUCTION STAFF

There are many people involved in making any play a success. As a matter of fact, when you see a play, you are only seeing a small percentage of the production staff. Read the job duties at the right and match them with the job descriptions to the left.

Producer - the highest authority in a play. Hires the director and often the director's staff. Also in charge of all the finances.

____

Director - the artistic mind of the show and the boss. Directs the actors, helping them to become the best they can be. Also advises the technical director.

____

Assistant Director - bridges the gap between the director and the cast and crew, especially when things get busy. Fills in any time the director is needed in two places at the same time. In school productions, usually the prompter too.

____

Prompter - the person whose main responsibility is to follow along in the script and give the actors their lines or stage directions when they need them. Also helps keep the director informed of where the actors are or need to be in the script.

____

Technical Director - in charge of all the technical crew members. Often works together with the director to design the set, lights, and sound if there aren't designers to do so. Makes sure that all technical aspects of the show please the director.

____

Stage Manager - in charge of the backstage area during rehearsals and performances. Has a script with all the cues and often makes cue sheets for the curtain, scenery changes, props, and even lights and sound. Makes sure that costume changes go smoothly. Prepares for any kind of backstage emergency.

____

Crew Chiefs - the people in charge of the individual crews. Specialists in their field, such as props, costumes, makeup, set, lights, or sound. Answer to the technical director. May have crew members working with them.

____

Grips - the backstage crew who fly scenery in and out.

____

Publicity Manager - promotes the show. Responsible for designing and printing posters and programs, sending out news releases, arranging all advertising.

____

House Manager - in charge of the "house"—areas where the audience enters, buys their tickets, takes refreshment, uses the restrooms, and sits to watch the show. Makes sure everything is clean, properly stocked, and comfortable. Crew members include ticket sellers, ushers, concessionaires, and even custodians.

____

If the show is a musical, a **Choreographer** will be in charge of the dance numbers and a **Musical Director** will coordinate the musical numbers.

____

Match the situation to the production staff member who is best suited to handle the situation (not the person who would tell someone to handle it).

1. *An actor forgets a line and needs help.*
2. *Some of the actors are being loud backstage during a rehearsal.*
3. *The wig bill is due.*
4. *An actor needs to be more emotional during a certain scene.*
5. *The director is sick and cannot attend rehearsal.*
6. *The stage manager cues a set piece.*
7. *A costume change is taking too long and the director wants it to run more smoothly.*
8. *The director is not happy with the way the lights looked in the last scene.*
9. *It is time to have the posters printed and hung throughout town.*
10. *One of the chorus members sprained her ankle, and a new girl must be trained in the songs and dances.*
11. *It is opening night and there are no paper towels in the lobby restrooms.*
12. *A prop is broken during rehearsal.*
13. *One of the actors cut his hand during the show and needs a small bandage before he returns to the stage.*
14. *The technical director has asked that a sound effect be sooner.*
15. *The director has quit and a new one must be hired.*
16. *An actor is saying the name of a city wrong.*
17. *The director needs a design for a small set piece but it is too late to hire a designer.*
18. *An actress needs an additional costume for the production.*
19. *A new usher is arriving late for every show.*
20. *The director thinks one of the actors might be saying a line wrong.*
21. *There is a production meeting at the same time as a rehearsal; the director must attend the rehearsal.*

shiny wood may convey a feeling of cleanliness, while a sandy, uneven, and smudged texture brings to mind filth. Which of the three textures below would you use if you were designing the set for a staged performance of The Grapes of Wrath? If you said C, the straw pattern, you think like a set designer! This texture is most likely to bring to mind images of farm life and drought.

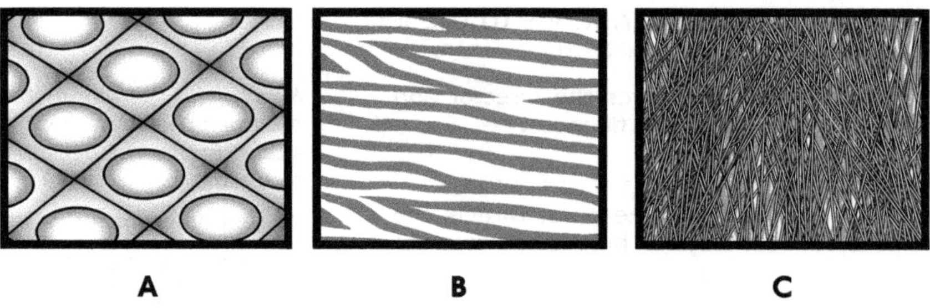

A B C

APPLYING STAGE MAKEUP

Stage makeup has several purposes. First, it helps to establish a character, such as adding age or a crooked nose. Also, it helps to define the actors' features so that the audience can see them and make out even subtle facial expressions. Finally, stage makeup can be corrective, evening the skin tone and making it look right under stage lights.

With just a basic knowledge of makeup application, you can supplement your knowledge with a good class, plenty of hands-on experience, plus books, videos, and online tutorials. Most students use the stage makeup provided by their school rather than less expensive street makeup. Theatrical makeup is more expensive, but the coverage is better and it is designed specifically for the stage. No matter the source of the makeup, each student should start by creating their own makeup kit.

Because your kit must move from home to stage and back again, it is important that it is mobile. Tackle boxes make great cases. They are sturdy and they have a convenient handle and several compartments. In the box on page 158 is a list of some items found in a typical student makeup kit.

Stage Makeup *Do's* and *Don'ts*

- Learn to apply your own make-up.
- Avoid sharing makeup, and never share mascara.
- Do not use makeup that causes severe skin reactions.
- Be ready to make changes to your application. What looks great in the dressing room may not look right under the stage lights.

Always start with a clean face. If you have never worn stage makeup before, do not wait until dress rehearsal to practice. Become familiar with putting on your own makeup long before you must do it with frayed nerves. Not only will you get the needed practice, but you will get to take inventory of your makeup kit, make any necessary purchases, and see how your skin reacts to the makeup.

After your face is clean, apply the foundation using a clean sponge. You will know when your foundation is done right when the entire face and neck are covered thoroughly and evenly and when all excess makeup is blended in. Cover even the lips and around the eyes.

Follow the foundation with facial powder with either a brush or a powder puff. This will set the foundation and give additional coverage.

Next, you will want to define your features. Of course, this will vary depending on your skin tone, your gender, and your character. However, a good rule of thumb is to highlight your existing features without making them appear fake. You will want to use shadow on your eyes, blush on your cheeks, and liner on your brows, eyes, and lips. Fill in your lips with a color that complements your skin tone and fits your character. If you have not yet powdered, do so now. This will tone down some of your

CONTINUED ON PAGE 158

NAME ______________________________ PERIOD ________ DATE ____________

CREATING MOOD PRACTICE

Choose one item from each box and write your choice on the line below the boxes. Once you have finished your selections, create the color, line, and texture schemes to complete the mood for your fictional play.

My play is about...
- a boy and a girl who fall in love but their love is forbidden.
- an evil landlord who is trying to collect on a debt by forcing a young widow to marry him.
- a deaf girl trying to overcome the odds to become a doctor.

It is set in...
- New York City in the wintertime during the Depression.
- the Old West.
- modern day Mexico in a beautiful village rich in heritage and with a bountiful crop.

The ending is...
- a happy one.
- a sad one.
- tragic.

My play is about ____

____.

It is set in ______________________________. **The ending is** ____________________.

Choose three colors that will be dominant in your color scheme. You may paint or color them or choose swatches of color from paint chips or magazines. Explain your choices based on what you know about your play and the colors.

COLOR 1	COLOR 2	COLOR 3

Select at least two samples each of texture and line either from actual samples (sand paper, cotton, etc.) or from pictures in magazines. Affix them below and explain your choices based on what you know about your play and the textures and lines. Use additional paper if needed.

TEXTURE 1	TEXTURE 2	LINE PATTERN 1	LINE PATTERN 2

makeup, so you may want to reapply lip color and anything that became muted. You can also spritz with a liquid makeup setting spray at this time. Finally, apply mascara after the optional setting spray since the spray will make some mascara run.

Watch stage makeup tutorials on YouTube. If your character is specific, seek videos featuring your character's makeup type as well as your skin tone. For example, search "lion makeup on dark-skinned actor" or "old age makeup for Asian male." This sounds overly specific, but makeup varies greatly from one skin tone to the next and from one ethnicity to another. Your research will be time well-spent. Because most theatres do not hire professional makeup artists, it is important that you learn to apply your own. It is a skill that will benefit you as long as you take the stage!

Various Shades of:	An Assortment of:	For Clean-up:	Other Items:
Foundation Eye Color Cheek Color Lip Color Cream Liners Pencil Liners Mascara Powder	Makeup Brushes Makeup Sponges Powder Puffs A smock for protecting clothes Hair bands or clips (even for short hair)	Cleanser Toner Cotton Balls Tissue Wash Cloth Baby wipes for removing makeup quickly	Shaver Shaving Cream Hair Brush and Comb Hair Spray Moisturizer Nail Polish Remover Deodorant Mirror

FINDING, MAKING, AND BUYING PROPS

Props are the things actors use onstage or the items used to dress the set. Hand props are those brought onstage by actors, such as a tray with cups, saucers, and a teapot that a maid carries onstage. Set props are placed on the set prior to the opening of the curtain. They are generally the things that decorate the "room" or the setting, such as a sofa, chair, lamp, and so on, but a set prop may also be a non-decorative item, such as a letter placed in a desk drawer to be found by a character at some point in the play. Body props are placed on an actor's body or costume to be used or referenced at some point during a performance. Say a character is wearing a tuxedo with a red flower in the buttonhole. He enters the scene and hands the flower to a beautiful passerby. The flower is a prop that must be placed onto the costume before each show.

In educational theatre, students in the production often bring props from home. The prop crew should keep record of who provides what props and who is responsible for returning the items. Some schools have well-stocked prop rooms from which many items can be taken. There are theatrical catalogs and specialty stores that sell props, such as realistic-looking rocks made of Styrofoam, swords made especially for stage combat, plastic food, etc. These mail-order companies stock some of the most commonly used items, but they are expensive. There are some companies that rent larger props like wooden foot bridges and Jack-in-the-boxes large enough for a live person. Again, these are expensive but a good option if you have little storage space. If you are doing a period piece (a show from a time period other than modern), you can find props at antique stores and vintage shops. Many of these stores will even lend them to you in trade for an ad in your program. You may also scrounge flea markets and garage and estate sales to cheaply supplement your prop closet.

At some point you will find yourself needing to make props. There are a number of materials that are lightweight, flexible or pliable, and easily available at craft or hobby stores.

- Plaster of paris is a great tool for molding props of detailed shape, such as statues.
- Chicken wire can be shaped into just about any form and covered with a variety of materials like papier-mâché to complete the project. Once dried, the papier-mâché can be painted.

- Tulle and netting are lightweight fabrics that are easy to manipulate into various shapes. They can be used to make inexpensive boas, wigs, tutus, petticoats, and more. It can also be used to make foliage, clouds, fog, water, and other set pieces and props with a wispy texture.
- Foam headliner is the padded fabric that lines the interior of the roof of your car. It comes in a variety of colors and can be stiffened with either paint or fabric stiffener.
- Styrofoam can be purchased in just about any size and can be shaped easily. Test your paints on a sample piece since many paints eat away at the foam or do not stick.
- Lightweight woods like balsa, Luan, and some pine are great prop-making materials, but they require special tools for cutting and shaping.
- Cardboard is easy to cut, shape, and paint. Take the two layers of corrugated cardboard apart, exposing the inner layer for a great textured material.

EXTENSION ACTIVITY

Choose one of the props below and tell how you would make it and the approximate cost. Use a clean sheet of paper and include a drawing of your design.

1. A cave large enough for a man to walk in and not be seen by the audience.
2. A floating cloud upon which an adult must sit. It should appear to drift on and offstage without assistance.
3. An elaborate crown that sparkles so much that it is almost luminous.

COSTUMING

The clothes worn by actors onstage are essential in setting the time in which the play takes place. They also help to establish each character's situation.

> *Imagine the last moments of the Titanic. See the deck of the ship as the last lifeboat is being lowered into the icy water below. It is cold and late at night in the early 1900s. As the great ship sits helpless, those who remain represent the unfortunate hundreds who are sure to perish. They include mostly poor men and members of the crew. Some wives refused to leave their husbands, and so scattered amongst the men are a few women. Life vests are testament that, despite the freezing waters, some still harbor hope of survival.*

Now imagine the cast of this play should your theatre produce it. It may include a football player, the short guy with glasses, the blossoming rock star with pink hair, the soccer player who injured her leg and is in a boot, and many others. They are average, modern-day kids, right? How can you convince the audience that this cast of teens is really the heroes and victims of the greatest story of the twentieth century?

Start by underlining every word in the italicized description above that indicates a costume need, then list them in the space below. There are at least seven.

____

____

____

As you can see, you will need costumes that represent the time period (early 1900s), the time of day (evening wear for the crew and wealthy), the temperature (cold), and the situation (many wore several layers both for warmth and because they hoped to save more of their personal belongings).

COSTUME CARE TIPS

- Safety pin loose items such as gloves to your costume between shows.
- When checking out your costumes the first time, make sure you have each item on your card. Keep a list of these for yourself so that you can account for each item every night.
- Keep a bottle of fabric deodorizing spray in your bag for freshening stale-smelling pieces.

Other hints in the description included icy water, poor men, crew members, some wives, and life vests. Think about your school producing *Titanic*. This scene is just one of many that would need costumes! Some shows are much simpler, with just a single costume needed for each character.

Most schools have access to costume closets stocked with various period pieces for both men and women. These costumes are often collected over the years from other shows. If your school is lucky enough to have several sewing machines and a supportive home ec teacher or skilled parent, the school can make any other costumes needed. With the concept of conversion costuming, you rarely have to start from scratch. Rather, find a book that explains how to convert an ordinary pair of men's slacks into knickerbockers or a thrift store blouse into a pirate shirt or peasant top. Of course, after the show, these too can be added to the costume closet.

For contemporary shows, many schools ask each student actor to provide their own costume, especially if they play a student and can just wear everyday street clothes. It is up to the technical director if these clothes will be kept at school as costumes for the run of the show or if the actors will be allowed to just wear them or bring them from home for each performance.

A popular, but very expensive, option for a period show, is to rent the costumes. Most large cities and towns have rental houses, which at least will save some money on shipping. Call in advance to make sure that the company near you has the items you need for the dates you need them. Once that is done, take measurements of each person needing costumes and what looks they require. Send the measurements to the rental company, and about a week before your show, you will receive your shipment of costumes.

Take extra care of every item, because many are vintage and very expensive. As of this date, prices average about $70 per costume, but replacement can be $300 or more.

Old prom dresses like this can be altered slightly, embellished, or remade to create stylish period costumes.

DESIGNING THE SET

Behind the set of a play, backstage visitors are often surprised at what they see. Many are surprised that the backside of the scenery is not similar to the front. Because scenery for plays must be lightweight, mobile, and durable while still resembling what it was intended to be, set pieces are built using non-traditional methods of construction.

Most sets are made up of flats (see pictures below), wooden frames with hinged braces on the back to help them stand. The fronts of the flats are often covered with a muslin fabric that is sized to fit and then painted. Sometimes set builders use paneling, Luan (pronounced loo-AHN, which is a thin sheet of plywood), or Masonite (a heavy, thin pressboard) to cover the frames. Once each flat is constructed, it can be painted to look like just about anything. The painted flats are placed together, creating the walls of a room or the exterior of a building. Sometimes the flats are joined together, but if they must be moved in the show, they are left freestanding with sandbags or weights to keep them from tipping over. Still, the backsides of sets are dark and the cast and crew must navigate the treacherous areas in big costumes or with heavy cables or props so sometimes set pieces fall over. Always prepare for the worst and use more sandbags than you think you need!

Many sets include backdrops, which are giant pieces of painted fabric hung from metal bars along the tops of the curtains. These are used for large indoor scenes such as libraries and for outdoor scenes such as a large city or a forest. These can be flown in and out using a system of ropes, pulleys, and weights called a fly rail. Theaters without fly rails rely on ladders and manpower to change the heavy backdrops.

To take the place of backdrops, projected scenery is becoming more and more popular because of its ease and lower cost. Projections can be done from the front onto a scrim, wall, or white sheet. For a different effect, projections onto a scrim can also be done from the back.

There are many other types of scenery, including two- and three-sided pieces on wheels that turn to reveal a new perspective. For example, if a high school was producing a show with three scenes, one in a library, one in a kitchen, and one in a garden, a prism set might be the best bet. Several tall, vertical, triangular pieces could be built and equipped with wheels for mobility. On the three sides of each prism, a piece of the three scenes would be painted. The space between the prisms become the doorways or entrances. With a quick turn of the prisms, the scene would change from a library to a kitchen, and then a garden. Once the basic structure of a scene has been built, the illusion can be completed by adding furniture, set props, and lighting.

The stage at Terrell High School before and after fourteen hours of work on the set.

LIGHTING AND SOUND

Greg Arp, a high school theatre teacher in Plano, Texas, says that while costumes, makeup, props, and set are all important, perhaps the most essential theatrical elements are lighting and sound. His productions certainly reflect a mastery of these production elements!

If an actor's primary objective is to be heard, then good sound is obviously a high priority. However, good sound is not just about microphones. It includes sound effects, recorded music or tracks if a live orchestra is not being used, and making sure the microphones can be heard over the live orchestra if it is being used. Sound technicians must also know how to operate high-tech equipment with dozens of cables, buttons, knobs, lights, and an infinite number of variables. They must have a very good ear so that they can sense when an actor's microphone needs to be tweaked. A good knowledge of acoustics is also important.

In smaller theaters and in some schools, actors do not use microphones. Instead, they rely on vocal projection to make sure the audience hears their voices. Also, because sound systems can be very expensive, many schools do not own them. Sound systems can be rented, and technicians can even be hired to run them. A less expensive option is to use home stereo equipment for sound cues or to have actors create sound cues offstage using hand-held devices.

What good is sound if the audience struggles to see the characters? The lighting crew must make sure that each lighting instrument is in good working order and that the lights are focused or aimed at the areas that need to be seen. Colored gels can be added or, if LED lighting is being used, a color may be selected from a menu of options to give the scene depth, as well as a time, place, and mood. Lighting is also important to ensure that the audience can see the actors' features and facial expressions and that the overall effect is what the director intended.

Most systems incorporate computerized digital boards, and each show must be programmed independently. Lights need to operate in groups to illuminate areas from several directions at once, and each light cue needs to be assigned a cue number. Once programmed, the light board operator must then follow along with the script at each rehearsal, cuing the light board. The operator also addresses whatever problems may arise during the show. For example, if an actor misses a line and that particular line was a light cue, the operator must adapt and adjust the lighting area to meet the needs of the show. The lamps, or bulbs, inside an instrument may burn out during a show, and the operator must know which instruments to use to illuminate the area in an emergency situation.

The benefits of LED lighting are that the lamps do not burn at a high temperature, they use less electricity, and the life of an LED lamp is significantly longer. The cost and use of LED fixtures have changed dramatically and the quality of light produced has improved. Many schools are transitioning from conventional light fixtures to LED fixtures for cost savings and low maintenance.

One of the great things about lighting is that it can eliminate the need for expensive scenery. Colored lights can be used to create a number of backgrounds such as sunsets, evenings, and just about any surrealistic setting imaginable. By adding a small, metal disk called a gobo to a conventional lighting instrument, stars, clouds, and other shapes can work with the color, creating wonderful effects. Intelligent lighting, or automated instruments that can be programmed to move, can make clouds appear to drift past a sun as it sets and stars begin twinkling on the horizon. Intelligent lighting can often be seen in large-scale productions and concerts and can be rented for school productions to create incredible lighting effects.

If your school is not equipped with the most advanced lighting technology or if you lack any kind of stage lighting, check into renting a portable system. If nothing else, consider making your own "coffee can lights" so that your actors can be seen.

Volumes have been written on lighting and sound, but theatre instructor Greg Arp suggests that the best way to learn is to work with an experienced lighting technician. If you are interested in working in this area of the theatre, Arp suggests seeking a technical internship from your local theatre.

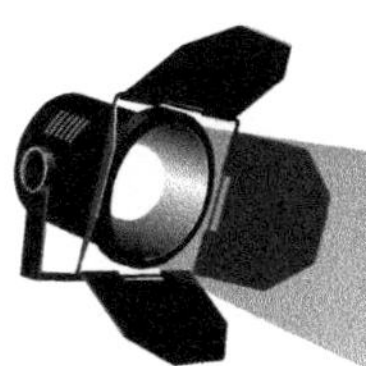

PRODUCING PLAYS IN NON-TRADITIONAL SETTINGS

A beautifully designed stage is a wonderful gift to the world of theatre. Actors and directors alike relish the idea of having the convenience and ease of the latest technology, the space for large dance numbers or a balcony scene, and a comfortable seating area for the audience. In an ideal stage setting, a workshop located near the stage allows both actors and crew to work simultaneously. When the lights need focusing, many facilities have practice rooms the same size and shape as the stage so that actors may work safely while the heavy equipment is lowered.

Unfortunately, the average school is not ideally equipped. Although many have stages, most were built on tight budgets. Sometimes there is not enough space in the wings for actors to await their cues. Often there is little to no storage space. Without storage, keeping stock set pieces, props, and costumes is difficult. There are a large number of schools with cafetoriums and gymatoriums—clever names for a combined auditorium and cafeteria or gym. Theatre students must juggle their rehearsal and performance schedules around sports, lunches, and gym classes. Regardless of the type of auditorium, most are the largest public gathering places in town, and they are used for a number of community events. All of this means sharing rehearsal and performance space and time slots and sacrificing storage space and technology.

There are also schools without any stage, so they think they cannot produce shows, if they even have a drama program at all. The truth is, a stage can be anywhere. In the Medieval period, actors traveled from town to town in pageant carts, which were wagons with fold-out stages. The wagons could be put together, forming a series of stages, or they could roll in and out in succession while the audience stayed put. When American theatre had its humble beginnings, amateur actors performed in courthouses, barns, and coffeehouses.

Not only is it possible to produce shows without a stage, but it is also a wonderful learning experience and a chance for you to develop your problem-solving skills. Plan on having more performances with fewer audience members due to the small spaces. Call on parents, woodworking classes, and community members to assist you. Here are some more ideas for producing plays in non-traditional settings:

- Host a dinner theatre play in a local restaurant's party room or your school cafeteria. Most publishers have scripts specifically for dinner theatre, where no stage is required beyond perhaps a head table, like at a banquet. Many of these shows are fun murder mysteries and make great fundraisers too!
- Perform in a park to take advantage of natural settings and lighting. You will need to rent cordless microphones so actors can be heard. The audience provides their own seating and admission is usually free. Ask for donations and sell concessions, and have a solid plan for bad weather.
- Ask your community theatre or another school if you can use their stage. Some churches also rent out their social halls or maybe you can even use the sanctuary so that the pulpit becomes the stage.
- Find a play with a setting that works with your present resources. For example, if you have access to a large barn, do a play that takes place at a farm. If your school's library would work, then choose a play with a school setting.
- Build a stage using a series of platforms and walls that can be taken apart and stored. Even if you lack storage, your parents may know of a local business that will store them for you, like a large warehouse or a building that has unused rooms.

VIRTUAL THEATRE

The term "virtual theatre" means that people are able to watch the performance of your show online. There are many ways this can happen, from livestreaming to posting a pre-recorded video on a website to performing live on a video conferencing site. Taking your theatre production "virtual" means you don't need much room for an audience, and you might not even need a stage at all!

If your performance space has limited room for an audience, you might consider livestreaming your staged performance so that additional people can be watching from home. This is especially nice for relatives who live out of town. However, first you have to find out from the publisher of the play if this is allowed. Some don't allow it, and the ones that do generally require an additional fee to be paid since you're reaching another audience.

You might also post a video of your staged performance on your school's website or on a site such as YouTube. The advantage of this is that people can watch it at their own convenience rather than at a specific time. Again, check the licensing agreement you have with the publisher. Many don't allow this, and the ones that do will definitely require additional royalty fees.

But what if you don't have a stage at all? In 2020, most theatres had to close worldwide because of a pandemic. Instead of cancelling their productions, some groups learned how to perform their show on a video conferencing site such as Zoom. As you can imagine, it's very different to put on a play without any performance space. Each actor is in their own house, yet they're all logged onto the same website at the same time to appear altogether on one screen. Performers can still appear in costume and makeup but there's less emphasis on sets or blocking. This style of performance is quite different and takes much rehearsal. While less than ideal, it is better than nothing when there's no stage available, whether for health or other reasons.

CHAPTER 8
THEATRE HISTORY

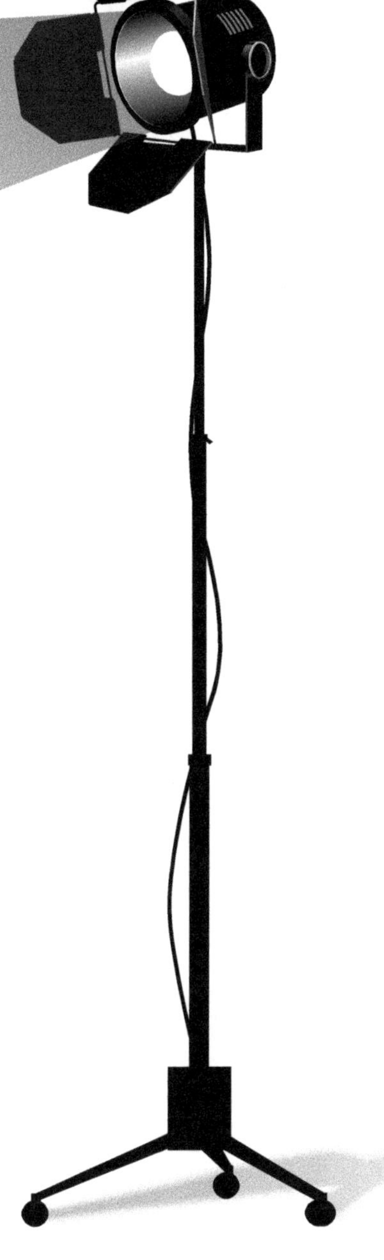

NAME ________________________________ PERIOD ______ DATE ____________

DAILY BELL WORK - THEATRE HISTORY

Answer each question as your teacher assigns it, using the space provided. Be sure to include the date.

1. Date: ________________

   What are some events the prehistoric people may have pantomimed in their early storytelling?

2. Date: ________________

   Imagine sitting around a prehistoric campfire listening to a story. What are some of the sounds and lights which may have naturally added to the drama of the story? How can these things be used to enhance drama today?

3. Date: ________________

   For the earliest writers, daily life was much harder. Paper and ink were sparse, and politics and religion threatened freedom of speech. Knowing this, write an entry from a fictional writer's diary describing the events of the day.

4. Date: ________________

   There was a great deal of disease during the medieval period. How might this have affected the traveling troupes of actors?

NAME ______________________________ PERIOD ________ DATE ______________

DAILY BELL WORK - THEATRE HISTORY

Answer each question as your teacher assigns it, using the space provided. Be sure to include the date.

5. Date: ________________

   Horseplay has long since been a source of enjoyment for audiences. Imagine a medieval performance of a morality play, a play about good and evil. What are some opportunities for the actors to engage in horseplay?

6. Date: ________________

   Commedia dell'arte used stock characters. These characters were the same in many plays, but the plot of each play varied. Today, the repetition of a character "type" in a performance is often referred to as a stereotype. List five or six stereotypes that are used in TV and film today.

7. Date: ________________

   Many commedia dell'arte plays used a plot in which a young man and woman are in love, but the girl's father is opposed. Can you think of film and TV plots that follow this popular pattern? List them.

8. Date: ________________

   Could you imagine a modern world in which people used Shakespeare's language? Why would this work or not work? Write your response in the language of a Shakespearean play.

NAME ______________________________ PERIOD ______ DATE ____________

DAILY BELL WORK - THEATRE HISTORY

Answer each question as your teacher assigns it, using the space provided. Be sure to include the date.

9. Date: ______________

   Throughout history, literature has been used to voice ideas about politics, religion, ethics, and social consciousness. In recent history, television, music, and movies have been added to the cause. Does the entertainment industry have a responsibility to exercise its power to influence society? Explain your answer.

10. Date: ______________

    Theatre has been outlawed several times throughout history, because it was believed to put bad thoughts in people's heads, which would then lead to bad behavior. Compare this theory to modern day beliefs that violence on TV and in video games leads to more violent behavior.

11. Date: ______________

    Theatre in the United States lacked its own identity until the early twentieth century when film was introduced and when stage plays began paving the way for American greatness. Write a diary entry from a young actor's actress's point of view as they see more opportunities in acting arise.

12. Date: ______________

    Should cartoons be considered art or are they just child's play? Explain.

NAME ______________________________ PERIOD ______ DATE __________

DAILY BELL WORK - THEATRE HISTORY

Answer each question as your teacher assigns it, using the space provided. Be sure to include the date.

13. Date: ______________

14. Date: ______________

15. Date: ______________

16. Date: ______________

THEATRE HISTORY TIME LINE

WITH INFLUENTIAL POLITICAL AND SOCIAL WORLD EVENTS

BC

c. 2560 BC: The Great Pyramid of Giza completed in Egypt.

2000 BC: Stone tablet depicting first known performance in Egypt.

c. 1800 BC: World's oldest surviving narrative, *Epic of Gilgamesh,* carved into The Old Babylonian tablets.

1000 BC: Greeks rebuilt their civilization after its collapse in the Late Bronze Age.

776 BC: First documented Olympic Games.

750 BC: Greeks learned the alphabet from Phoenicians; Homer composed *The Iliad* and *The Odyssey* about the Trojan War and the Fall of Troy.

c. 563-400 BC: Buddha born in India.

551-479 BC: Life of Chinese philosopher and politician Confucius.

534 BC: Thespis became the first "actor," stepping from the traditional chorus to act as an individual.

c. 529 BC: Greek thinker Pythagoras developed theories about music, physics, and mathematics, including what became recognized as the Pythagorean Theorem, a fundamental of geometry.

525-456 BC: The life of Aeschylus, Greek playwright, "Father of Tragedy."

509 BC: Roman Republic established.

508 BC: Cleisthenes introduced democratic governance in Greece, ushering in the Classical Period, a high point in culture and the arts that lasted until the death of Alexander the Great in 323 BC.

496-406 BC: The life of Sophocles, Greek playwright, author of *Antigone, Oedipus Rex*, and *Electra*.

490 BC: Greeks repelled Persian invaders at the Battle of Marathon.

480-406 BC: The life of Euripides, Greek playwright, author of *Medea, Hippolytus*, and The *Trojan Women*.

445-385 BC: The life of Aristophanes, Greek playwright, "Father of Comedy."

438 BC: Construction of the Parthenon completed.

431-404 BC: Greek city-states Sparta and Athens fought the Peloponnesian War.

c. 400 BC: Women first allowed to attend the theatre.

342-290 BC: The life of Menander, prolific Greek playwright of comedies. Only *Dyskolos* survives today.

336-323 BC: Macedonian King Phillip II conquered Athens to control Greece. Upon Phillip's assassination, his son Alexander the Great led armies to conquer Persia, Syria, Egypt, and parts of India before dying suddenly in Babylon.

335 BC: Greek philosopher Aristotle penned *Poetics*, the earliest surviving work of dramatic theory. A year later he opened the Lyceum.

254-184 BC: The life of Plautus, Roman playwright, who adapted most of his works from earlier Greek plays.

221-206 BC: China, unified under Emperor Qin Shi Huang. Construction began on The Great Wall.

190-158 BC: The life of Terence, Roman playwright.

146-60 BC: Roman conquest of Greek regions introduced Greek philosophy and theatre to Rome.

146 BC: Rome destroyed Carthage bringing an end to the Third (and final) Punic War, and to the Carthaginians.

44 BC: Assassination of Julius Caesar signaled the end of the Roman Republic and the beginning of the Roman Empire.

3 BC-65 AD: The life of Seneca, Roman philosopher, statesman and playwright, author of *Medea, Thyestes*, and *Phaedra*.

First through Tenth Century AD

33 AD: Crucifixion of Jesus of Nazareth.

43 AD: Romans conquered Britain.

79 AD: Pompeii is buried in twelve feet of volcanic lava and ash.

80 AD: Built amid a nearly 200-year stretch of prosperity and relative peace known as Pax Romana, the Roman Colosseum was completed, allowing for seating of up to 80,000 spectators.

300-645 AD: During the Yamoto period, Japan organized a unified state and established ties to mainland Asia.

c. 350 AD: Indian poet Kālidās composed *Shakuntala*, which would become one of the first Sanskrit works translated into English.

390 AD: Theodosius the Great declared Christianity the official religion of Rome.

410 AD: Visigoths shocked the world by conquering Rome, the "Eternal City."

476 AD: Flavius Odoacer revolted against and replaced Emperor Romulus Augustulus, effectively ending the Western Roman Empire.

500-800: The lotus of Roman power shifted to Constantinople in the East, in what's now known as the Byzantine Empire, and Western Europe fell into disrepair. Since Christians generally opposed theatre, it became virtually non-existent in Western Europe.

574-622: Emulating China, Shōtoku Taishi began to transform Japan, centralizing the government, emphasizing a bureaucracy of merit, and reverence for Buddhism and Confucianism.

630: Mohammed entered Mecca in triumph; two years later the Qu-ran was completed.

710-794: Japanese court built a new capital in Nara modeled upon Chang-an in China; emperors are Shinto chiefs. They adopted Buddhism hoping that its teachings will bring peace and protection.

711: The Umayyands conquered the Iberian Peninsula spreading Islam to Europe. The Islamic state, or caliphate, would by 750, rule from the Atlantic Ocean in Northern Africa in the west into modern day Afghanistan in the east.

794-1185: In Japan, the Imperial Court moved to Heian-kyō (now Kyoto) to escape domination of Nara's Buddhist establishment.

800: Frankish king Charlemagne crowned the first Holy Roman Emperor.

800-1000: Height of Byzantine Empire, hub of world commerce and industry.

c. 800: Chinese accidentally created gunpowder.

900: The Roman Church resurrected theatre by introducing religious performances to Easter services.

c. 950: Hrosvitha, a member of German nobility, wrote six plays based on Terence's comedies but featuring religious figures. Her work became the first known example of Western dramatic theatre since the Classical Era.

Eleventh Century

1002: Japanese court women produced the best literature of the era; Murasaki Shikibu's *Tale of Genji* is the world's first novel.

1046: Pope Gregory VII took steps to unify the Roman Church and strengthen its rule in Rome.

1066: William I, Duke of Normandy, conquered England.

1095-1271: The Crusades: first of many attempts by the Roman Church to reclaim the Holy Lands from Islamic rule.

Twelfth Century

1100-1220: Troubadour poetry spread throughout France, Spain, and later Italy. Themes mainly concerned chivalry and courtly love.

1100-1300: Origin of universities in Western Europe.

1140-1260: Aristotle's works translated into Latin.

1150-1500: Gothic style in architecture and art.

1192: Shogun Minamoto no Yoritomo overthrew the Taira Emperor, establishing what would become 675 years of military rule in Japan.

Thirteenth Century

1206-1260: Genghis Khan unified tribes of Mongolia and conquered territory throughout China, the Middle East, and as far northwest as Poland. His empire expanded after his death and then contracted after Islamic Mamluks defeated Mongols at the Battle of Ain Jalut.

1212: Spanish victory over Muslims at Las Navas de Tolosac.

1215: King John of England signed the Magna Carta, which would inspire those seeking liberty for hundreds of years hence.

1271-1295: Life of Italian merchant and explorer Marco Polo, whose stories in *The Travels of Marco Polo* inspired Europeans to build trade routes eastward.

1290: Mechanical clock invented.

Fourteenth Century

1314: Italian statesman and poet Albertino Mussato wrote *Ecerinis*, the first tragedy written since Roman Times.

1315-1317: Famine choked Northern Europe.

1337-1453: England and France fought the Hundred Years' War, which helped establish their respective national identities.

1347-1350: The Black Death, a pandemic of the bubonic plague, killed between 75-200 million people in Europe, Asia, and North Africa.

1387-1400: Geoffrey Chaucer penned *The Canterbury Tales*.

Fifteenth Century

1415: Italian inventor Giovanni Fontana wrote *Bellicorum instrumentorum liber* (Book of Instruments of War), an illustrated book about military technology, including a discussion of rockets and torpedoes.

1429: Joan of Arc led French to free Orléans from the English. She was burned at the stake two years later.

1440: Johann Gutenberg invented the printing press. This technological breakthrough allowed the spread of information faster than ever before.

1450-1600: The Renaissance Period: the rediscovery of classical Greek philosophy led to a new, expanded way of thinking, that reverberated through all facets of life.

1453: Ottomans captured Constantinople, leading to the end of the Byzantine Empire. The Ottomans would control Constantinople (later named Istanbul) until the end of the First World War in 1917.

1455-1487: Civil wars, called the Wars of the Roses, were fought between the House of Plantagenet and the House of Lancaster over the English throne.

1467-1477: The ten-year-long Ōnin no Ran (Onin War) brought disintegration of the central government in Japan and led to the beginning of the Sengoku period.

1475-1564: The life of Italian sculptor, painter, and poet Michelangelo di Lodovico Buonarroti Simoni.

1476: Ulrich Han first printed a book containing music, in Rome.

1478: Catholic leaders Ferdinand II of Aragon and Isabella I of Castile implemented the Spanish Inquisition, which would persecute Jews, Muslims, and (so-called) heretics for the next 300 years.

1483-1520: Life of Italian painter and architect Raphael Sanzio de Urbino; his best known work is *The School of Athens* in the Vatican.

1492: Italian explorer Christopher Columbus crossed the Atlantic Ocean and landed in the Bahamas, opening the door for the European colonization of the Americas.

c. 1495: Writing of *Everyman*, a morality play whereupon one's good and evil deeds are tallied by God in a ledger. It has seen many adaptations since.

Sixteenth Century

c. 1500: Transatlantic Slave Trade: Sailing from Europe, merchants kidnapped and enslaved men, women, and children from Western Africa.

1503: Italian painter, scientist, and engineer Leonardo da Vinci began painting the *Mona Lisa*.

1504: Michelangelo completed *David*, a masterpiece in marble.

1508-1512: Michelangelo painted the ceiling of the Sistine Chapel in Rome.

1516: In the Venetian Republic, a law limited Jews to San Girolamo Parish, establishing "Ghetto Nuova" as the first ghetto in Europe.

1517: Martin Luther nailed his *Ninety-five Theses* to All Saints' Church in Wittenberg, beginning the Protestant Reformation—and eventually splitting Western Christianity into Catholics and Protestants.

1519: Spanish conquistador Hernán Cortés met Aztec leader Montezuma in one of the world's largest cities Tenochtitlan (modern Mexico). Within two years, the Aztec Empire was destroyed.

1520-1566: Under Suleiman the Magnificent's reign, the Ottoman Empire entered its "Golden Age," expanding to include over 25 million people.

1521: Voyage of Magellan completed with his crew, having circumnavigated the globe.

1524: Italian diplomat and writer, Niccolò Machiavelli published *La Mandragola*, a five-act satire.

1533-1603: Life of Queen Elizabeth, long-reigning ruler of England, patron of the arts.

1542: Pope Paul III established the Roman Inquisition to combat Protestantism.

1543: Firearms introduced in Japan by shipwrecked Portuguese.

1549: Christianity introduced in Japan by Frances Xavier.

1551: Commedia dell'arte gained popularity in Italy and Western Europe.

1562-1589: Catholics and Huguenots Protestants fought the French Wars of Religion.

1564-1593: Life of Christopher Marlowe, English playwright best known for tragedies, wrote *Hero and Leander, Tamburlaine the Great,* and *The Tragical History of Doctor Faustus.*

1564-1616: Life of William Shakespeare, English playwright, wrote *Hamlet, Romeo and Juliet, Macbeth, Othello, A Midsummer Night's Dream*, and many more.

1568-1600: Oda Nobunaga started the process of reunifying Japan after a century of civil war, laying the foundation for modern Japan.

1570: The Elizabethan masque, an elaborate combination of dance, music, and costumes performed for aristocrats, debuted.

1572-1637: Life of English poet and playwright Ben Jonson, author of *Every Man in His Humour, The Alchemist,* and *Bartholomew Fair.*

1576: The first Elizabethan playhouse, The Theatre, opened in London.

1581: First ballet performance, "The Comic Ballet of the Queen," staged in Paris.

1582: Pope Gregory XIII instituted the Gregorian Calendar.

1588: English defeated the Spanish Armada.

1590-1681: The Golden Age of Spanish Theatre: Spain produced four times more plays than the English during their theatrical renaissance. Playwrights included the prolific Lope de Vega, soldier and priest-turned-playwright Calderón de la Barca, and former nun Juana Inés de la Cruz.

1594: The foremost Elizabethan theatrical company, Lord Chamberlain's Men, formed with William Shakespeare as its chief playwright and Richard Burbage as its most famous actor.

1598: Edict of Nantes allowed Protestants in France to practice their religion in peace.

Seventeenth Century

1600: The Globe Theatre staged its first production, *Julius Caesar.*

1600-1750: Baroque Period: encouraged by the Catholic Church to counter the simplicity of Protestant art, Baroque art used color, detail, and movement to create works that would create a sense of awe in the viewer. Later baroque works, known as rococo, became even more extreme and ornamental.

1605: Spanish writer Miguel de Cervantes published *Don Quixote, Part I*, considered among the most important novels ever written.

1607: Englishman John Smith founded the first colony of Virginia at Jamestown.

1609: Italian inventor and scientist Galileo Galilei published *The Starry Messenger*, a compilation of his astronomical discoveries.

1611: The King James Bible was published.

1613: Fire destroyed the Globe Theatre.

1620: Pilgrims sailed to America on the Mayflower.

1622-1673: Life of French writer and actor Molière (born Jean-Baptiste Poquelin), author of *Tartuffe, The Misanthrope,* and *The Learned Women*.

1631-1700: Life of critic, poet, and playwright John Dryden, England's first Poet Laureate.

1631: Mt. Vesuvius erupted, destroying everything around the volcano and killing between 3000 and 6000 people.

1636: Harvard College founded in Cambridge, Massachusetts.

1637: The first public opera house, the Teatro San Cassiano, opened in Venice.

1639-1699: Life of French playwright Jean Racine, a tragedian, who wrote *Andromaque, Phèdre,* and *Athalie*.

1640-1689: Life of Aphra Behn, one of the first English women to make her living as a writer.

1641-1716: Life of English dramatist William Wycherley, writer of *The Country Wife* and *The Plain Dealer.*

1642-1660: English Civil War: Tensions between King Charles I and Parliament erupted in armed hostilities. Throughout the war, the Puritan majority ruled, and Parliament closed all theatres in England.

1643: Molière founded Illustre Theatre in Paris.

1651: First public comedy house opened in Vienna, Austria.

1653-1725: Life of Japanese dramatist Chikamatsu Monzaemon, innovator in bunraku and kabuki, writer of *The Courier for Hell,* and *The Love Suicides at Amijima.*

1660-1710: The Restoration Period: The reopening of English theatres led to a theatre boom that welcomed women to the stage, diversity to the audiences, and popularized comedy.

1661: Lincoln's Inn Fields, London's largest public square, opened.

1662: The English Royal Patent mandated that women perform female theatrical roles.

1663: The Theatre Royal, Drury Lane, London, opened.

1665: *Ye Bare and Ye Cubb*, on record as the first English-language play presented in the colonies in the colony of Virginia.

1665-1666: Bubonic plague killed an estimated 100,000 people, nearly a quarter of all Londoners.

1673-1841: Golden age of kabuki theatre: Japan starts to flourish with kabuki and bunraku theatre and broader access to education and books.

1681: Professional female dancers appeared in Paris for the first time.

1687: English physicist, theologian, and astronomer Isaac Newton published *Mathematical Principles of Natural Philosophy*.

Eighteenth Century

c. 1700: Italian Bartolomeo Cristofori invented the first modern piano.

1705: The Queen's Theatre opened in London.

1707-1793: Life of Italian playwright Carlo Goldoni, founder of modern Italian comedy, author of *Servant of Two Masters* and *The Mistress of the Inn*.

1711-1785: Life of Kitty Clive, English actress.

1714: Italian composer Antonio Vivaldi (1678-1741) became the impresario of the Teatro Sant' Angelo, helping popularize opera throughout Europe.

1720-1860: Life of Italian playwright Carlo Gozzi, revitalized commedia dell'arte by bringing an intense satirical edge to it.

1728-1774: Life of Irish writer Oliver Goldsmith, author of the plays *The Good-Natur'd Man* and *She Stoops to Conquer*.

1730: *Romeo and Juliet,* performed in New York, is the first play by Shakespeare to be presented in America.

1737: One of the largest theatres in Europe, Teatro di San Carlo, connected to the Royal Palace, opened in Naples.

1737: English Parliament passed the Stage Licensing Act, which required all public performances to be examined and, if necessary, censored by the government. It would exist in some form until 1968.

1748: The excavation of Pompeii, buried by a volcano eruption 1700 years earlier, inspired what will become known as the Neoclassical Period (1750-1815), an embrace of Greeco-Roman ideals, of simplicity and grace. In theatre that meant decorous plays, acted very broadly, with meticulous costumes and sets.

1749-1803: Life of Italian dramatist and poet Vittorio Alfieri, the founder of Italian tragedy.

1750: First resident theatre company established in New York City.

1751-1816: Life of English playwright, poet and politician Richard Brinsley Sheridan, author of *The Rivals, The School for Scandal, The Duenna,* and *A Trip to Scarborough*.

1751: The Virginia Company of Comedians, the colonies' first professional theatre company, opened a temporary playhouse in Williamsburg, Virginia.

1766: The first permanent American theatre building, Philadelphia's Southwark Theatre, was built.

1766-1839: Life of American playwright, actor and historian William Dunlap, author of over 60 plays and the encyclopedia *History of the Rise and Progress of the Arts of Design in the United States*.

1768: Italian naturalist Lazzaro Spallanzani proved that boiling and sealing food products will keep them free of microorganisms, thus creating modern-day canning.

1775-1783: The American Revolution, prompted by Americans drafting the Declaration of Independence, declaring their intent to secede from Great Britain.

1784: Pierre Beaumarchais' comic play, *Marriage of Figaro,* premiered. It was later developed into an opera composed by Mozart and a libretto written by Lorenzo Da Ponte.

1788: United States ratified The Constitution. The next year, George Washington became the first US president.

1789-1815: The French Revolution and Napoleonic Wars: Inspired by the ideals of liberty, equality, and fraternity, civilian insurgents stormed the Bastille, a symbol of monarchy rule in Paris. Political struggle, wars with other European nations, the beheading of King Louis XVI, and the abolishment and reestablishment of the Catholic Church culminated in dictatorial rule by a council known as the Directorate—which was subsequently commandeered by Napoleon Bonaparte. Napoleon and the *Grande Armée* engaged nearly every other European power in battle until his ultimate defeat at the Battle of Waterloo. The peace, negotiated at the Congress of Vienna, re-drew the borders of Europe, and established the British Empire as the world's foremost power.

1791-1861: Life of French playwright Eugène Scribe, who developed the "well-made play," a popular, though criticized genre that emphasized rigid plot structure and entertainment over didactic-ism.

Nineteenth Century

1800s: Using simple characterization and exaggerated emotions, melodrama—as written by August von Kotzebue and René Charles Guilbert de Pixérécourt—dominated French theatre.

1800-1890: Born from Germany's sturm und drang movement, Romanticism offered artists and thinkers an opportunity to focus on emotion and individualism instead of the encroaching modernity and industrialization.

1808: German writer Johann Wolfgang von Goethe published *Faust, Part I*.

1816: Philadelphia's Chestnut Street Theatre became the earliest gas-lit playhouse in the world.

1821-1881: Life of Russian writer Aleksey Pisemky, who introduced psychological realism to playwriting, authored *A Bitter Fate* about serfdom.

1828-1910: Life of Russian author Leo Tolstoy, author of the novels *War and Peace, Anna Karenina*, and the play *The Power of Darkness*.

1837: A London theatre first used Thomas Drummond's limelight, similar to today's spotlight.

1848: Germans Karl Marx and Friedrich Engels published *The Communist Manifesto*, a political document describing society through the lens of class struggle.

1854-1900: Life of Irish poet and playwright Oscar Wilde, author of *The Importance of Being Earnest*.

1856-1950: Life of British/Irish playwright George Bernard Shaw, writer of *Man and Superman, Pygmalion,* and *Saint Joan*.

1859: English naturalist Charles Darwin published *On the Origin of Species*, founding the science of evolutionary biology.

1861-1865: American Civil War: After the election of President Abraham Lincoln and fearing the abolition of slavery, seven southern states seceded from the United States and formed the Confederate States of America. During the war, Lincoln issued The Emancipation Proclamation, freeing slaves in rebel territory. Shortly before the war's end, John Wilkes Booth assassinated Lincoln.

1861: The transcontinental telegraph linked the east and west coasts of the United States.

1868-1912: Emperor Meiji transformed Japan from a feudal island nation into an industrialized world power.

1869: The Transcontinental Railroad was completed at Promontory Point, Utah.

c. 1870s: Realism: Following the trend of French painters, dramatists sought to represent life as it appeared. In realistic plays, characters spoke without verse or meter, sets were dressed as if they were actual locations, and psychological considerations motivated characters' decisions.

1871: To create *Thespis*, English producer John Hollingshead introduced librettist W.S. Gilbert to the composer Arthur Sullivan. Gilbert and Sullivan would write 14 comedic operas, including *H.M.S. Pinafore, The Pirates of Penzance,* and *The Mikado*.

1879: Eadweard Muybridge invented the zoöpraxiscope, forerunner to the motion picture projector.

1879: *A Doll's House*, Henrik Ibsen's drama about the repression of women, premiered at the Royal Theatre in Copenhagen.

1881: The first building lit entirely by electric light, The Savoy Theatre, opened in London's West End. The West End and New York City's Broadway would become the pinnacles of professional theatre in the English-speaking world.

1884: European leaders divided Africa into imperial colonies at the Berlin Conference.

1884: First elevator stage constructed at the Budapest Opera House.

1888-1953: Life of American playwright Eugene O'Neill, whose *Long Day's Journey into Night* is considered one of the best American plays of the 20th century.

1891: First public demonstration of a working motion picture at Thomas Edison's lab.

1896: First US movie theaters opened in Buffalo, NY and New Orleans, LA.

1897-1975: Life of American playwright Thornton Wilder, who authored *Our Town* and *Skin of Our Teeth*.

1898: Spanish-American War: The United States conquered Cuba, destroyed the Spanish navy in the Pacific and decisively ended the Spanish Empire.

Twentieth Century

1900: At Broadway's Casino Theatre, *Floradora* opened, introducing the Floradora sextet, a forerunner to the modern day chorus line.

1902: Los Angeles built its first movie theatre.

1904: Anton Chekhov's play of modern realism, *The Cherry Orchard*, premiered at the Moscow Art Theatre.

1904-1905: The Russo-Japanese War pitted Japan and Russia against one another for competing colonial claims in Korea. Japan surprised the world with their resounding victory.

1905-1984: Life of American dramatist Lillian Hellman, who wrote *Foxes* and *Toys in the Attic*.

1907: Broadway producer Florenz Ziegfeld Jr. introduced his legendary theatrical revue Ziegfeld Follies.

1908-1981: Life of novelist and playwright William Saroyan, who authored *The Time of Your Life, My Name Is Aram,* and *My Heart's in the Highlands*.

1909: Russian theatre actor and director, Konstantin Stanislavsky, introduced "method acting," whereupon a character's internal decisions influence their external action.

1911-1983: Life of American playwright Tennessee Williams, writer of *The Glass Menagerie, A Streetcar Named Desire, Cat on a Hot Tin Roof, Sweet Bird of Youth*, and *The Night of the Iguana*.

1913: Featuring an all-black cast, the large scale musical *Darktown Follies* helped launch Harlem as an African-American cultural center.

1914-1918: World War I: Ultimately, the war resulted in nearly thirty million casualties, the end of all empires in Europe (Germany, Russia, Austria-Hungary, Ottoman), and ongoing political upheaval.

1915-2005: Life of American playwright Arthur Miller, writer of *All My Sons, Death of a Salesman, The Crucible*, and *A View from the Bridge*.

1917: Russian Revolution: The March and October Revolutions in Russia deposed Emperor Nicholas II and instigated the Russian Civil War that would end in 1922 with the founding of the USSR, led by Vladimir Lenin.

1920: *Beyond the Horizon*, Eugene O'Neill's first full-length play, won the Pulitzer Prize, marking the beginning of modern American drama.

1920: The African-American migration to northern cities ignited the Harlem Renaissance.

1921: America's first resident professional theatre, The Cleveland Playhouse, opened.

1927-2018: Life of American play- and screenwriter Neil Simon, author of *Biloxi Blues, Come Blow Your Horn,* and *The Odd Couple*.

1927: Jerome Kern and Oscar Hammerstein's musical *Show Boat* debuts on Broadway. Despite heavy themes involving race and tragic love, *Show Boat* is chock-full of song, dance, and spectacle, marking Broadway and musical theatre as a distinctly American art form.

1927-1949: Chinese Civil War: The Chinese Nationalist Party (CNP) and Communist Party (CPC) of China vied for control of the largest country on Earth, suspending hostilities during Japan's invasion from 1937-1945. Ultimately CPC, led by Mao Zedong gained control of mainland China, while CNP took residence in Taiwan.

1929: The New York Stock Market crashed and the Great Depression followed.

1930: American Jean Rosenthal pioneered stage lighting and the idea of it as a career.

1930-1965: Life of Lorraine Hansberry, whose *A Raisin in the Sun* tells of an African American family's experience in Chicago.

1932: Radio City Music Hall opened in New York City. The "Showplace of the Nation" is home to the leggy dance company, The Rockettes.

1935: Opening in Boston, George Gershwin's *Porgy and Bess* featured a cast of classically trained African-American actors.

1937-1945: World War II: The war and its consequences ultimately killed up to 85 million people, including 6 million Jews and 5 million others killed in the Holocaust. It also led to the formation of the United Nations, established the United States and the Soviet Union as the world's only superpowers, and kicked off a nuclear standoff between them, called the Cold War, that would last until 1991.

1950: Frank Loesser, Joe Swerling, and Abe Burrows's *Guys and Dolls* debuted on Broadway.

1952 - : Life of American playwright Beth Henley, winner of the Pulitzer Prize for her play *Crimes of the Heart*.

1954: In Brown v. Board of Education, the US Supreme Court declared that segregated schools were unconstitutional per the 14th Amendment.

1955-1975: Vietnam War: In one of the Cold War's proxy wars, the US and the USSR took opposing sides in a civil war in Vietnam. In the US, where the government conscripted young men to fight, the war became a cultural flashpoint.

1957: Leonard Bernstein, Stephen Sondheim, and Arthur Laurents brought *West Side Story* to Broadway. Its complex and enduring music, societal themes, and extended dance numbers still influence Broadway theatre.

1957: Both the Tony Award and the Pulitzer Prize are awarded to Eugene O'Neill's *A Long Day's Journey into Night*.

1957: The Soviet Union launched Sputnik 1 into Earth's orbit.

1963: Civil rights leader Martin Luther King Jr. delivered the "I Have a Dream" speech in Washington DC, a call for racial equality. Five years later he was assassinated.

1968: The controversial rock musical, *Hair*, opened on Broadway. *Hair* dealt frankly with profanity, drug use, and sexuality and notoriously included a nude scene.

1969: The United States landed astronauts Neil Armstrong and Buzz Aldrin on the moon with pilot Michael Collins delivering them back to Earth.

1982: Andrew Lloyd Webber's *Cats* opened. It became Broadway's longest running play until it was surpassed by Webber's own *Phantom of the Opera*.

1989: The Fall of the Berlin Wall led to the reunification of Germany (which had been split since 1945) and symbolized the end of the Cold War. The USSR dissolved two years later.

1989: English engineer Tim Berners-Lee wrote the code for the World Wide Web, the first web browser, allowing what had started as an U.S. Department of Defense project, ARPANET, to develop into a global network serving 3.2 billion people and counting.

1991: In the Gulf War, America forced Iraqi dictator Saddam Hussein's armies out of Kuwait.

1998: Osama Bin Laden and his Al-Qaeda terrorist network destroyed two American embassies in eastern Africa.

Twenty-First Century

2001: Al-Qaeda terrorists hijacked four planes and used three of them to bring down the World Trade Center Buildings in New York City and to attack the Pentagon; the fourth plane, which is thought to have been heading for the White House, crashed in an empty field.

2003: US invaded Iraq a second time to eject tyrannical leader, Saddam Hussein, and to install a democratic system of government.

2008: Barack Obama became the first African-American President of the United States.

2012: Simon Stephens' play, *The Curious Incident of the Dog in the Night-Time,* premiered on Broadway, showcasing an autistic main character.

2013: Scientists successfully cloned human stem cells.

2015: Lin Manuel Miranda's musical *Hamilton* debuted on Broadway featuring an ethnically diverse cast portraying America's founding fathers and music drawn from hip hop and R&B.

2020 - : A worldwide pandemic shut down countries around the globe. In the US, state-at-home orders forced businesses, schools, and theatres to close. Broadway shows and national tours were cancelled, as schools and amateur theatres scramble to create Virtual Theatre.

THE FIRST PERFORMANCES

The history of theatre is closely tied to that of the world. When a writer sat down with his quill and paper, he looked around him for inspiration. He may have written about the wars, the politicians, the attitudes of the day, or some young couple he heard about from the friend of a friend. Even if what he wrote about was fantasy, in most cases it was still based on those things to which he had been exposed. Years later, we read these old plays and stories, and we get a glimmer of an idea as to what life must have been like for the people in that place and time.

Before the written word, stories were told around campfires. Imagine a darkened hillside with tall trees rustling in the wind. The golden glow of a campfire sends shadows creeping up the sides of the cliffs. The cool wind carries the howl of a distant wolf pack barely heard over the crackling of the fire. You are a tribal person sitting in the dirt, dressed in skins, waiting for the day's hunt to come off the fire. While you wait with the rest of the tribe, the huntsmen act out the pursuit of the hunt while the youngest in the group, costumed in the skin of the kill, plays the role of the prey.

The story starts low; the group has come upon a bison grazing in a small enclosed valley. Quietly they surround it, spears propped and ready. Someone steps on a stick, alerting the beast to the danger. He darts, and the chase begins. One of the young huntsmen finds himself cornered by the frightened animal, who has lowered his head in preparation for the attack. He snorts and paws the dusty ground, then hurls his huge body at the hunter. With no place to go, the man thrusts his spear, hitting right between the shoulder blades, but it is not enough to stop the charging beast. He braces himself for certain death, when out of the brush a barrage of spears and bodies bring the giant animal down.

It is possible that many stories like the one above were enacted for thousands and thousands of years. Topics probably included great hunts, the harvest, feats of heroism and bravery, and perhaps even some love stories. Eventually, music may have been added, such as the beat of a drum. Dancing would almost certainly accompany that. However, we have no written records of these performances, just speculation.

The first record of a theatrical performance was found on a stone tablet in Egypt dating back to about 2000 BC. It describes a three-day performance arranged by and starring I-Kher-Wofret of Abydos. Proving that violence is not a new theatrical device, this performance used realistic battles and high ceremony to reenact the murder, dismemberment, and resurrection of the god Osiris.

ANCIENT GREEK THEATRE

Despite the Egyptian performance, the Greeks are generally credited with giving theatre its start. About 1,400 years after the reenactment of Osiris's demise, Greeks were paying tribute to their gods as well. In honor of Dionysus, the god of wine and fertility, and to commemorate his death, the Greek chorus danced around an altar, upon which a sacrificed goat was placed. They sang a song called a "goat song," or tragos. It is from this word that we get the word "tragedy."

The chorus played an important role in Greek theatre, keeping the audience informed as to what was happening onstage. However, in 534 BC, a man named Thespis did something no one had done before. He broke away from the chorus and held dialogue with them onstage. This action made him history's first actor. Today, actors are called thespians, named after this trendsetter.

The development of the stage was one of the greatest contributions the Greeks gave to the theatre. Originally held with semicircular hillside seating, the addition of wooden and eventually stone seats added a sense of sophistication for the all-male spectators. By the time women attended the theatre around 400 BC, the theatre could seat over 15,000 people. It was large enough that those seated at the back had a hard time hearing and seeing. The large masks worn by the actors helped with this.

Elaborately decorated with exaggerated characteristics, these masks added size to the characters, making them easier to see. There were about thirty different types of masks worn by Greek actors onstage. Believed to be introduced by Thespis, the masks were made of lightweight wood, cork, or linen and served many purposes. Because the plays had few actors (one early on and three later), the masks allowed one actor to play several roles. Also, because women did not act, these devices allowed men to play women's roles. Unfortunately, the masks prevented the actor's own facial expressions from being seen, so he had to rely on his voice to make his characters real and interesting.

The area where the chorus danced was called the orchestra. Behind the acting area was a small hut-like building called a skene (pronounced SKEE-nee). This served as the actors' dressing rooms. Eventually, several stories and wings were added to the building, the front of which was used to paint scenery. The roof was used as an acting area for the gods. If the gods needed to fly, a crane-like device called a machina (MAH-kee-nah) would hoist them into the air. The term "deus ex machina" refers to the plot device originating in the Greek theatre in which a problem was resolved quite unexpectedly when a god would appear from nowhere and save the day.

GREEK PLAYWRIGHTS

We still have many of the plays that were written by ancient Greeks, but because of the passage of time, many are fragments with the remainder of the play lost. It is believed that many great works are gone altogether. Despite their age, these classic plays remain popular, many based on universal and timeless themes that never seem to lose popularity.

There were many playwriting competitions held in ancient Greece in which playwrights competed for prizes and public favor. The playwright of the competing play not only wrote the text itself, but he composed the music, choreographed the dances, directed, and often held the lead role. The entries were divided into two categories: tragedies and comedies. It was not uncommon for the great playwriting competitions to require writers to submit four plays in the tragic category—three tragedies and a satyr play or a trilogy and a satyr play—all related in theme. However, to compete for the comedy prize, a writer only had to submit one play. Hidden within these two types of Greek plays was a third type—the tragicomedy or satyr play. This was a tragic story with comic undertones.

Aeschylus: Aeschylus (ES-kil-us) is the earliest known Greek playwright. Born in about 525 BC, he is believed to have written around Ninety plays. Of those, only seven survive in their entirety. He is also credited with having the only surviving trilogy—the *Oresteia*, three closely connected tragedies, first performed in 458 BC. Because of his long career and the influence of his writings, we can see the development of Greek theatre in his works. His earlier plays have choruses of fifty and only one actor, but his later works show the trend of his contemporaries toward the smaller chorus and several actors. He died in 456 BC; his tombstone did not mention his career as a writer.

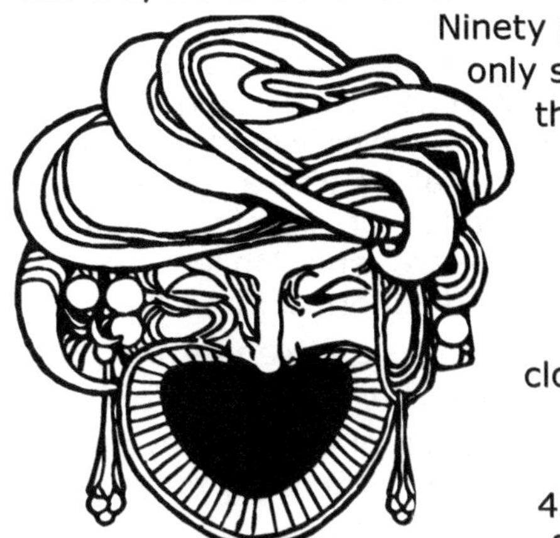

A mask much like the ones worn by Ancient Greek actors. Note the large hollow mouth which allowed actors to project their voices.

- His most famous plays are *Agamemnon, The Libation Bearers*, and *The Eumenides*.
- He is often referred to as the "Father of Tragedy."
- He wrote about the choices men make and the consequences that follow.

Sophocles: During Aeschylus's lifetime, the younger playwright Sophocles (SOF-uh-clees) began his career. He wrote between 90 and 110 plays, but only seven survive today. He is said to have won the playwriting prize eighteen times! He compared the power of the gods to the importance of humanity, believing that humans possess god-like qualities that make them want to change fate. In a time when it was considered impious to doubt fate, Sophocles armed his characters with the power to challenge the paths the gods set before them. Many believe that this was what made his characters some of the greatest to take the stage.

- His most famous plays are *Oedipus* (EH-di-pus) *the King, Oedipus at Colonus, Electra*, and *Antigone* (an-TI-guh-nee).
- He was born in 497 BC and died in 406 BC.
- Along with Shakespeare, he is considered one of the greatest playwright of all time.

Euripides: The last great writer of Greek tragedy, Euripides (yoo-RIP-eh-dees) was born in 484 BC and died in 406 BC, the same year as Sophocles. He wrote about ninety plays, eighteen of which survive. Winning the prize only five times, it wasn't until after his death that his plays truly earned public appreciation. His exploration into the psychology of the individual, especially women, as opposed to the larger public issues taken on by his predecessors, seemed to be a bit too modern for his time.

- His most famous plays are *The Trojan Women, Medea*, and *Hippolytus*.
- His *Cyclops* is the only complete satyr play known to exist.
- He originated the use of the prologue to summarize the play for the audience before the action.

Aristophanes: Born in 448 BC, Aristophanes (air-uh-STAH-fuh-nees) is the only writer of ancient Greek comedy whose works still exist in whole today. However, it is believed that like his tragic counterparts, three-fourths of his works are missing or incomplete. Furthermore, because his comedy is based on a type of wit that gets lost in translation, modern audiences have less appreciation than those of his day. He died in 380 BC.

- His most famous plays are *The Birds, The Clouds*, and *The Frogs.*
- His plays made fun of the leaders of Athens, the gods, and even his playwright counterparts.

ROMAN THEATRE

Unfortunately, theatre did not flourish in Rome as it did in Greece. Instead, it veered sharply into a bawdy and decadent form of base entertainment that appealed to the audience's sense of vulgarity, sensuality, and violence. Featuring obscene mimes, drunken horseplay, and dancers in meager bikinis, the performances rarely had plots that dealt with challenging issues. With plays based on the lowest aspects of human nature, it is not surprising that actors' reputations suffered. This set a trend that would take centuries to change.

The Romans had great impact on the architecture of the theatre, bringing it closer to the stages of today. The theatres were built in a flat area instead of on a hillside, as had been done in neighboring Greece. The once-open space was replaced with an elaborately decorated wall that surrounded the seats and the stage. Because the chorus was no longer being used, the orchestra became obsolete, making the stage the central focus. The stage was positioned high off the ground with tiers of benches at the front and the scaenae frons (an elaborately decorated wall) at the rear. Later stages even featured curtains that could be closed at the end of a scene, awnings for the audience, concessions, and even perfumed water mists to cool and deodorize the audience on hot days.

There were two great writers of Roman comedy, Plautus and Terence. During their time, Rome lacked the elaborate stages that were yet to come (as were the large audiences). Later, Seneca, a writer of larger-than-life dramas, wrote plays that are better read than produced. Consequently and ironically, none of Rome's esteemed playwrights benefited much from the great architecture of the period.

Plautus: Twenty of this writer's plays are still in existence today, all written between 205 BC and 184 BC. Because they were not published in his lifetime but left in the hands of actors, it is believed that a great deal of Plautus's work has been modified. Regardless, at a time when the audience seemed indifferent to political issues, his plays found popularity and longevity. Like Terence and Seneca, he borrowed his plots from the Greeks, but he added a personal touch to them that made them uniquely his. He used poetic devices (which would get lost in translation), proving that he was an artist, and the subsequent imitation of his plots by later writers like Shakespeare and Molière, prove that he had a profound historical impact.

- His most famous plays are *Menaechmi (The Twin Brothers)* and *Amphitryon*.
- Despite his borrowed plots, his plays paint an accurate picture of life in his times.

Terence: Born an African slave to a Roman senator, Terence exhibited brilliance early in life, winning for himself an uncommon education and his subsequent freedom. Using applicable plots and a universal dialogue, he had less popularity with the Roman audiences who craved buffoonery and vulgarity. Born in 195 BC, he wrote all six of his plays by the age of twenty-five. He left Rome under suspicion of plagiarism, never to return. He died in 159 BC.

- His most famous plays are *Andria* and *The Eunuch*.
- He was paid 8,000 sesterces for *The Eunuch*, which was the greatest sum ever paid for a comedy at that time.

Seneca: A native of Cordoba in Spain, Seneca was born in 4 BC with fragile health. As a result of this and the fact that his father was a great speaker, he devoted himself to the spoken word and to the study of philosophy. He was banished in AD 41 by Claudius, but recalled by the Empress Agrippina eight years later and employed as her son Nero's tutor. Seneca was devoted to the family for many years, but when mother and son broke apart, he sided with Nero, drawing up all of his state papers and defending him in his mother's murder. After falling out of favor with the new ruler, Seneca committed suicide in AD 65 rather than be subjected to a more humiliating death.

- His most famous plays are *Octavia, The Phoenician Women*, and *Hercules*.
- His plays are generally considered closet dramas, plays that are meant to be read rather than acted.

NAME ____ PERIOD ______ DATE ____________

EARLY THEATRE REVIEW

1. How did the earliest performances probably originate?

2. A stone tablet is the first record of a theatrical performance in ___________ , dating back to about ___________ BC. It describes a _______ -day performance by ______________________ of Abydos.

3. Describe the Egyptian performance.

4. The __________________ are credited with the origins of theatre, despite the earlier Egyptian performance. They were honoring their god of wine and fertility, __________________.

5. The word tragedy comes from the Greek word _________ which means _______ _______.

6. The __________________ played an important role in Greek theatre, keeping the audience informed of the action onstage. In 534 BC, __________________ stepped from the chorus and engaged in dialogue with them, making him the first actor. It is from him that we get the word "thespian," a term used today which means actor.

7. What was the purpose of the Greek mask?

8. Define:

   a. Orchestra

   b. Skene

   c. Machina

9. __________________ is the earliest recorded Greek playwright. His trilogy, _______, is the only one known to have survived. He is often referred to as _______ __________________ of __________________. His plays include __________________, the __________________ __________________, and the __________________.

10. __________________ is often referred to alongside Shakespeare as the greatest writer of all time. He took a great risk when he gave his characters the power to change the __________ the __________ had put before them. He wrote __________________ the King, __________________ at Colonus, __________________, and __________________.

11. __________________ earned public appreciation for his writings only after his death. While other playwrights of the time dealt with larger ___________ ___________, he explored the psychology of __________________, especially women. His __________________ is the only complete satyr play known to exist.

12. ___________________________ is the only writer of Greek comedies whose plays are still known to exist today. His plays, which included ____________, ____________, and ____________, poked fun at Athenian leaders and the gods at a time when free speech was not well accepted.

13. Roman performances included a great deal of mime, dancing, and __________________.

14. Roman playwrights included ex-slave __________________, __________________, and the Spanish-born __________________.

MEDIEVAL THEATRE

The period from about AD 500 to AD 1500 is known as the medieval period in theatre history. Following the decline in popularity of the theatre in Rome and the demise of respect for actors, the period to follow was a difficult one for the theatre. Traces of performances such as mimes, acrobatics, and singing can be found, but anything structured like a play remained difficult to find until later. Like the Greeks who used plays to worship Dionysus, Christians would introduce theatrical performance to the church and its mostly illiterate congregation as a means of worship and teaching the gospel.

Initially, priests used liturgical chants during the Mass to teach those who could not read about the events in the Bible. Eventually these chants grew into more elaborate productions that, because of the limited space within the church, had to be moved outdoors. Because of the content and probably due to the texts being in Latin, the players were priests, nuns, and choirboys. However, at some point the plays were translated from Latin, which opened the doors for commoners to participate.

Medieval drama has a language all its own. The following are some terms from the period:

Miracle and mystery plays—plays based on the saints' lives and Bible stories.

Passion plays—plays based on the last week in the life of Christ.

Mansion—a series of acting stations in a line, including heaven, Pilate's house, Jerusalem, and hell's mouth.

Guilds—groups of tradesmen with a common trade (bakers, goldsmiths, etc.). Each guild would be responsible for part of a Bible story that, when combined with other guilds' performances, made a cycle. Each guild competed with the others to see who could produce the most elaborate story.

Cycle—the combined stories produced by the guilds.

Morality play—similar in theme to miracle and mystery plays, yet more concerned with the principles taught by Christianity rather than stories from the Bible.

Masque—a spectacular play glorifying the nobility.

Pageant cart—a two-storied cart that doubled as a stage (with the underside being a dressing room). During a cycle, the carts would move from place to place, each producing the same story over and over again for different segments of the audience, which would remain stationary and enjoy each performance as it moved through.

Some groups not associated with the church began performing miracle and mystery plays, but they drew criticism from those with church ties, and it was not long before their performances were repressed. However, these pioneers do represent the first acting companies and were later recognized and patronized by the nobles.

Despite the seriousness of the message and the religious content of medieval theatre, the performances continued to appeal to the audience's sense of horseplay. Any opportunity for silliness and buffoonery was seized. Noah's wife became a nag, and the Tower of Babel lent itself to unlimited comic dialogue. However, the audience's favorite figure to take comic pokes and humorous stabs at was Satan. The gleeful attitude with which he and his assistants handled hell's business gave the viewers a frighteningly enjoyable incentive to be good. Even after the scenes in which Satan was a part of the story, his assistants, adorned in horrific masks, continued to pop into the story for no apparent reason other than to keep the audience amused with feats of acrobatics and farcical miming. Perhaps this is why even today one of the most prolific symbols of the medieval period continues to be the jester.

Other aspects of the medieval stage that helped to draw in large audiences were the complicated technical devices and special effects. For example, trap doors were hidden in the raised stages so that characters could appear from nowhere or disappear. Some troupes had cranes to fly angels in. However, one of the most fascinating devices had to be the contraption known as hell's mouth. With a moving jaw, real flames, and smoke bellowing from its bowels, the device would consume those characters who were too evil for heaven. It took seventeen men to operate one such device.

MEDIEVAL PLAYS

- *The Second Shepherd's Play*—a secular play about a clever scoundrel named Mak who steals a sheep, hides it in a crib, and passes it off as his son.
- *Everyman*—an allegorical (utilizing strong symbolism) morality play in which Everyman is summoned to meet Death, appear before God, and seek salvation. Other characters include Five Wits, Fellowship, Kindred, Discretion, Beauty, Strength, Knowledge, and Good Deeds.

Christians would introduce theatrical performance to the church and its mostly illiterate congregation as a means of worship and teaching the gospel.

MEDIEVAL REVIEW

1. Medieval plays were based mainly on stories from the ________________ and the lives of saints. They were called ________________ and ________________ plays.

2. Plays based on the last week of Christ's life, called ________________ plays, are still performed today.

3. Similar to the above were ________________ plays, only these taught the difference between right and wrong rather than about Christianity itself.

4. A ________________ was a glorious spectacle performed for the benefit of the nobility.

5. Despite the seriousness of the message, medieval plays still had a lot of __________ ________________________________.

6. Name two medieval plays:

RENAISSANCE THEATRE

Perhaps the busiest period in theatre history was the Renaissance era, which began early in the fourteenth century and continued until the start of the seventeenth century. Renaissance means "rebirth," which is fitting since this is the time when theatre sought new life after being almost non-existent for many centuries following the Roman period and then forbidden for all but clergy during the medieval period.

The Renaissance in theatre had its first sparks of life in Italy with a rediscovery of the classics. The pageant carts that had been the medieval standard were not suited for more modern plays, so new playhouses were constructed. Ancient Roman theatres became the model from which the newer facilities were built. New theatres, however, progressed even further with the addition of a proscenium arch—the arched wall above the stage opening. Furthermore, the Italians began using fabulously painted scenery that reflected the development of the visual artistry flourishing in southern Europe at that time. Despite the new designs, the revived classics, which were suited to a more educated audience, lacked mass appeal.

The most famous contribution of the Italian Renaissance was a style of theatre called commedia dell'arte. Although it has its roots in the classical styles of the Greek and Roman plays and even in the burlesque style of the medieval period, this new development was unique unto itself. Aside from a basic plot and subplot and stock characters, the entire performance was improvised, including brief comedic moments called "lazzi" and longer comedic scenes called "burle" that often involved practical jokes. The actors experienced a freedom—or responsibility—previously unheard of. The necessity for dancing and singing, acrobatics, mime, juggling, and quick wit meant that actors had to be skilled as well as intelligent and talented.

The plays were performed by traveling companies, which were groups of performers who worked together continually as an organization. Because of the mobile nature of the new style, portable stages again became a necessity.

THE CHARACTERS OF COMMEDIA DELL'ARTE

The colorful characters of commedia dell'arte may be its most outstanding legacy. Each was based on a stock personality, a lot like modern-day typecasting. As a matter of fact, many of the stock characters used during this period are still used today. During the Italian Renaissance, the actors who played each of these roles were specialized and would play the same character from one play to the next and even throughout their lifetime. Unless there was a major change in appearance due to age, actors did not change characters.

The Innamorati, a pair of young lovers, generally provided the main plot. In most cases, they wanted to marry, but the heroine's father or guardian opposed it. The heroine was referred to as the "inamorata" and her lover as the "inamorato." They were attractive characters, beautifully dressed, and they did not wear masks. Today, when a boy and girl are in love, they are said to be "enamored," which derives from the same root word.

The heroine's maidservant, Columbina, was the Fontesca or shrewd female servant. She was flirtatious and witty. She and the various comic menservants and nagging housekeepers, called Zanni, were responsible for keeping the action dynamic yet always returning to the plot. They were often paired similarly to Laurel and Hardy—one bright and mischievous and the other fumbling and foolish. Some familiar stock servants were Arlecchino, Pulcinella, and Pedrolino. Brighella, who often played the female counterpart to the manservant, was brash, rude, and could make men blush.

The heroine's father or guardian, Pantalone, was a worldly lover and contrary parent who struggled against a rebellious child. He was overbearing and a bit sneaky.

Il Capitano was a braggart soldier who acted like a brave hero, but eventually the audience learned that he lived in constant fear of his own shadow.

Although commedia dell'arte eventually died out, its influences remain strong and undeniable. Even today, characters similar to those stock characters of the period are still seen in plays, movies, and TV shows, as is the typical plot. Can you think of some modern-day characters from TV, movies, or plays that might have been influenced by commedia dell'arte?

With the exception of The Innamorati, commedia dell'arte actors often wore masks to designate their character. These half masks were often made of leather and included exaggerated features.

RENAISSANCE THEATRE OUTSIDE OF ITALY

Besides the Renaissance in Italy, theatre continued to develop elsewhere in Europe. Traveling troupes and players went from town to town performing smaller plays, while more well-known companies were invited to play in the great castles.

In Spain, Miguel de Cervantes was busy writing the famous novel *Don Quixote*, which over the centuries became the inspiration for many plays, including the musical *Man of La Mancha*. Lope de Vega and Pedro Calderon de la Barca are famous Spanish playwrights from the Renaissance period.

With the support of the government, theatre flourished in France. Some famous plays include Pierre Corneilles' *Le Cid* and Jean Racine's *Phaedra*. Perhaps France's most famous playwright of the late Renaissance period was Molière, who lived from 1622 to 1673. Several of his comedic plays, such as *The Miser, Tartuffe, The Misanthrope*, and *The Imaginary Invalid* are still performed and enjoyed today.

ELIZABETHAN THEATRE

The Renaissance spread through Europe to England and brought about a new type of theatre there, Elizabethan theatre. Named after Queen Elizabeth I, whose reign started in 1558, she was a patron of the arts. The Elizabethan era produced many great plays and playwrights, three of whom stand above the rest: Christopher Marlowe, Ben Jonson, and William Shakespeare.

Elizabethan drama flourished after England conquered the Spanish Armada in 1588, resulting in a burst of patriotic confidence and national identity. At this time in history, performers sought the patronage of wealthy noblemen. This protected their reputations while providing funding and stability. In the eyes of their fellow actors, those with noble endorsement were considered "legitimate." Any actors who failed to secure this royal support were considered rogues. That's why the idea of "legitimate" theatre has its roots in the Elizabethan era.

During the Elizabethan period, women were not permitted to act because the stage was considered unladylike and unsuitable for women. Instead, young boys who possessed smaller frames and higher voices played the women's parts. While we might consider this practice odd today, it was all that the players of the time knew, so it was considered quite normal and acceptable.

The plays of Shakespeare, Marlowe, and Jonson drew large, boisterous crowds seeking out bawdy entertainment, especially in the lower levels where admission was the cheapest. However, in the early 1600s, theatre started to veer off in a new direction, and a different kind of play started to emerge. This new form of entertainment, called court plays, was geared to a more intellectual audience—royalty and nobility. Unlike the raucous plays of Shakespeare and Jonson, the newer works by Francis Beaumont and John Fletcher were subtle and sophisticated.

Civil war erupted in 1642, and the theatre again went into hibernation. Banned by the Puritans, most of the stages were destroyed or allowed to deteriorate. England would not see a new theatre until 1660.

THE ELIZABETHAN STAGE

Playhouses in the Elizabethan period were round or octagonal with three levels or galleries of seating, with the best seats reserved for those who could afford the highest fee. Those with little money stood in the pit, the bare dirt floor in front of the stage; thus, they were called groundlings. Those willing to pay the greatest fee could sit on the stage.

The actors performed on a platform stage with trap doors throughout, but because the theatre itself was open, little scenery was used. Likewise, there was no stage lighting, so plays were performed in the daylight. The stage did have a partial roof, however, and it was elaborately decorated to resemble the nighttime sky with stars and the zodiacs surrounding the sun, thus its name—the heavens. The wall behind the actors resembled the exterior of a building. An area above the stage could be used as an additional acting area, but more often it housed the musicians. Above that was storage, and at the top of the building was a flag to inform the public of an impending performance.

ELIZABETHAN PLAYWRIGHTS

Christopher Marlowe: Born in 1564 in Canterbury and dying when he was just 29 years old, Marlowe is credited with the introduction of blank verse. He acted and wrote under the patronage of Lord Admiral. He was hailed as the greatest English dramatist until Shakespeare began to make his mark. This comparison and eventual dethroning led to a fierce rivalry between Marlowe and Shakespeare. His unfortunate death after being stabbed in a tavern brawl may have robbed history of a literary genius before his prime.

- His most famous plays are *Tamburlaine the Great, The Jew of Malta, Edward II*, and *The Tragical History of the Life and Death of Doctor Faustus*, commonly called *Doctor Faustus*.
- Although born the same year as Shakespeare, Marlowe began his theatre career at an earlier age.

Ben Jonson: Jonson (1572-1637) is considered the first real English comic. He was born the son of a clergyman and educated at Westminster School by William Camden, the great classical scholar. However, he was deprived a university education by a domineering stepfather who made him an apprentice bricklayer. Eventually he joined the army, serving in Flanders, and returned to England in 1592, marrying Anne Lewis.

Painfully aware of his lack of higher learning, Jonson became bitter and often found himself in trouble. His rebellious nature was also evident in his work, as he wrote and spoke with little self-censoring.

- His most famous plays are *Volpone, The Alchemist*, and *Every Man in His Humour.*
- He was imprisoned several times.

William Shakespeare: The Bard (1564-1616) has almost undisputedly been granted the title of the greatest playwright ever. He produced a huge and diverse collection of works—154 sonnets and 37 comedic, tragic, and historical plays. The popularity of his historical plays was likely fueled by the patriotic sentiment in England at the time.

Shakespeare was born in Stratford-on-Avon and moved to London in 1594 in order to act. Shakespeare's acting company built The Globe Theatre in 1599, and many of Shakespeare's most famous plays were performed there. In 1613, a theatrical cannon in a production of *Henry VIII* misfired, starting a fire that caused the entire structure to burn down. It was rebuilt the following year.

- His most famous plays are *Romeo and Juliet, Hamlet, Macbeth, Othello, A Midsummer Night's Dream, King Lear, The Taming of the Shrew,* and *The Tempest.*
- None of his plays was published until after his death; consequently, many dispute the purity of the plays, arguing that they were altered by the playhouses that kept them over the years.

NAME ______________________________ PERIOD ______ DATE __________

RENAISSANCE & ELIZABETHAN THEATRE REVIEW

1. Renaissance means ______________. This applies to the theatre, because it was almost non-existent after it was forbidden to all but clergy in the medieval period.
2. Commedia dell'arte plays were performed by traveling ______________, or groups that worked together as organizations.
3. Commedia dell'arte characters were __________ characters, meaning the actors played the same ones from play to play despite the changing plots.
4. The young female character, the heroine, was called the __________ and her young male lover the __________. Her father was called ______________, and her maidservant was the ______________. The braggart soldier was named ______________.
5. Describe the influence of commedia dell'arte on modern-day entertainment:
6. Queen ______________ was the ruler during the period of English theatre that produced greats like Shakespeare, Marlowe, and Jonson. To be considered a part of legitimate theatre, actors and writers sought the patronage of wealthy ______________.
7. During this period, wealthy spectators sat in the galleries while the poor, or ______________, stood in the pit. The wealthiest were seated on the ______________.
8. ______________ was the most rebellious of the three great Elizabethan playwrights. He wrote __________, ______________, and ______________.
9. Marlowe is credited with the introduction of __________ ______________. He was considered the greatest English playwright until ______________ plays became more popular, dethroning Marlowe. Marlowe wrote ______________, ______________, ______________, and ______________.
10. William Shakespeare has almost undisputedly been dubbed the greatest playwright of all time. He wrote __________ plays and __________ sonnets. None of his plays were published until ______________, creating a theory that they may have been written by others or perhaps altered by those who had been charged with their keeping.
11. List five of Shakespeare's plays:
12. During the Elizabethan Period, ______________ were not allowed to act. Their roles were played by ______________.

THE ENGLISH RESTORATION AND LATER THEATRE

In 1642, the Puritans closed all theatres in England, and for eighteen years, theatre stayed shuttered under the rule of the Puritan leaders. The Restoration started when Charles II was "restored" to the throne in 1660. Theatre was again made legal, and with it came many important innovations. The old theatres had fallen into ruin, and the old plays did not fit the mood of the times and the people. There was an opportunity for a fresh start, and two men were assigned to supervise the task: Thomas Killigrew and William Davenant. They were both experienced playwrights, and Davenant was rumored to be Shakespeare's son by a mistress. He is even attributed with what could be called the first English opera.

The major tool used to restore theatre was the English Royal Patent of 1662, which mandated that women perform female roles. It also endorsed the theatre as "useful and instructive." Only two theatres, the Drury Lane and the Covent Garden, received official sanction, but this was still a huge improvement from the past two decades. Other small theatres popped up, but only those with official sanction were considered legitimate.

During this time, the architecture of the playhouse also saw important changes. For one, they had complete roofs for the first time, which allowed for more elaborate scenery and stage mechanics. They also added lighting by elaborate chandeliers, and the orchestra moved to the front of the stage. The back wall was replaced with shutters that rolled back and forth in grooves in the stage. This allowed for multiple scene changes. The audience sat on level floors, and to help them see the actors, the stage was tilted slightly toward them. Because the actors were performing on an incline, they had to move "up" and "down" the stage. Consequently, we now use the terms upstage and downstage despite most modern theatres being level. Like the slant of these Restoration theatres, upstage is furthest from the audience; downstage is closest.

There were several famous writers from the period: William Wycherley (1641-1716), who wrote *The Country Wife* and is known for being a comic trendsetter; William Congreve (1670-1729), who is considered a master of comedy and wrote *Love for Love* and *The Way of the World*; and George Farquhar (1678-1707), who wrote *The Beaux' Stratagem*.

The greatest actor of the Restoration was David Garrick. Unlike many who specialized in either comedy or drama, Garrick was equally good at both, and his natural movement and line delivery set him apart from the previously stiff style. Besides acting, he wrote plays, and he made an important innovation in stage lighting when he blocked the lighting instruments from the audience's view. One of the most famous actresses of the period, Peg Woffington, was Garrick's mistress for many years. She rebelled against the gender-biased Elizabethans by effectively portraying men's roles.

Within five months of each other in 1808 and 1809, both the Drury Lane and the Covent Garden burned to the ground. This symbolized the end of an era, and as new buildings were built to replace them, a new period of theatre emerged.

Teetering between the Restoration and the period to follow were Richard Brinsley Sheridan and Oliver Goldsmith. Sheridan (1751-1816) wrote *The School for Scandal* and *The Rivals*. Goldsmith (1728-1774) was a "one-hit wonder" with his play *She Stoops to Conquer*.

Starting in the 1870s, W.S. Gilbert and Arthur Sullivan produced fourteen operas, the most famous being *H.M.S. Pinafore, The Pirates of Penzance*, and *The Mikado*, which are all still extremely popular. Oscar Wilde gave us the delightful *The Importance of Being Earnest.* However, it is George Bernard Shaw (1856-1950) who dominated the late nineteenth and early twentieth centuries. Many rank him next to Shakespeare as one of England's greatest playwrights. A philosopher of sorts, Shaw used his writings as vehicles to voice his theories on humanity and intellect. His most famous plays are *Arms and the Man, Saint Joan*, and *Pygmalion*, from which the musical *My Fair Lady* was fashioned.

AMERICAN THEATRE

The American colonies were under strict puritanical control in the 1600s, and theatrical performances were outlawed. Viewing dramatic or comic plays was thought to negatively influence the behavior of the young and lead to maliciousness. Laws were passed prohibiting any such entertainment, and when the actors persisted, the audience was targeted with fines for viewing the "devilish acts." We know that amateur companies produced plays, but due to the lack of newspapers and public records, little is known about them. There is even some documentation of professional actors touring with amateur groups, but due to laws prohibiting these performances, there is little physical evidence.

In the early to mid-1700s, ideas began to change. Elegant balls became popular recreation for the wealthy. Tantalizing stories of the glamour of the English stage arrived with each docking ship. The settlers began to feel the void impressed upon them by a government fearful of self-expression. As rebellious attitudes grew, so did the acceptance of new ideas. Subsequently, many plays were produced, probably by amateurs, but it is impossible to say when or where the first professional American performance took place. Many were performed in courtrooms or coffeehouses, anywhere the actors could find room. At times the overcrowding led to fighting or even riots. New laws sought to keep stage plays out, but the people won their freedom, and American theatre was born.

There were few American-written plays at that time. Whether amateur or professional, the tried and true works of Shakespeare and other British writers became the staple of the local actors. The first American theatre was built in Williamsburg, Virginia in 1716, but its existence was a short one when its mortgage was foreclosed in 1723. It was later used to produce amateur college performances.

Theatrical families were not uncommon overseas, and in the mid-1700s they began appearing in the colonies. It was easier and less expensive to travel and produce plays as a family; all resources were readily available. Each family member had a special trade and several stock roles. Of course, there had to be some actors from outside the family, but where the company branched, another family often developed as actors married actors. Their children, who were exposed at an early age, naturally gravitated to acting careers. One of the most prevalent of these families was the Hallams. Young Lewis Hallam Jr. made his debut at the age of twelve with a single line, but he became so overcome by stage fright that he ran from the stage in tears before he could utter a single word. His stage fright in check, his reign on the American stage spanned fifty years until his death in 1808.

Another American theatrical family, the Barrymores, bridged the gap between early American theatre and modern film. Irish actor John Drew traveled to the states in 1846 and married actress Louise Lane. They had three children, and their daughter, Georgiana, married Irish actor, Maurice Barrymore. Their famous children—Lionel, Ethel, and John Barrymore—became some of the stage's first "household names." John was arguably one of the most acclaimed American actors of his generation and the grandfather of Drew Barrymore, a favorite current movie star both in the United States and around the world. What do you think her great-great-grandparents would say if they could see one of her movies?

Even as it grew and strengthened, American theatre lacked its own identity. Companies capitalized on European plays until the early twentieth century when writers like Eugene O'Neill, Thornton Wilder, and Tennessee Williams emerged. At the same time, however, Hollywood was becoming the center of the film industry for the world, somewhat overshadowing the development of the American stage.

AMERICAN PLAYWRIGHTS

The twentieth century brought an explosion of American playwrights, truly defining theatre in the United States both on and off-Broadway. The Pulitzer Prize in Drama started in 1917 and recognizes annually the best play or musical dealing with American life.

The plays listed below are just a sampling of some American playwrights' more recognizable titles. Plays that have won the Pulitzer Prize are indicated with an asterisk.

Eugene O'Neill**	1888-1953	*Beyond the Horizon** *Mourning Becomes Electra*	*The Iceman Cometh* *Long Day's Journey into Night**
Oscar Hammerstein II	1895-1960	*Oklahoma* *South Pacific**	*The King and I* *The Sound of Music*
Thornton Wilder	1897-1975	*Our Town** *The Skin of Our Teeth**	*The Matchmaker*
Lillian Hellman	1905-1984	*The Little Foxes* *Watch on the Rhine*	*The Searching Wind*
William Saroyan	1908-1981	*The Time of Your Life**	
Arthur Miller	1915-2005	*All My Sons* *Death of a Salesman**	*The Crucible* *After the Fall*
Tennessee Williams	1911-1983	*The Glass Menagerie* *A Streetcar Named Desire**	*Cat on a Hot Tin Roof** *The Night of the Iguana*
Neil Simon	1927-2018	*Barefoot in the Park* *The Odd Couple*	*Brighton Beach Memoirs* *Lost in Yonkers**
Edward Albee	1928-2016	*Who's Afraid of Virginia Woolf?* *A Delicate Balance**	*Three Tall Women**
Lorraine Hansberry	1930-1965	*A Raisin in the Sun* *Les Blancs*	*Fences** *The Piano Lesson**
Sam Shepard	1943-2017	*Buried Child** *A Lie of the Mind*	
August Wilson	1945-2005	*Ma Rainey's Black Bottom* *Jo Turner's Come and Gone*	
David Mamet	1947-	*Glengarry Rose** *Speed-the-Plow*	
Christopher Durang	1949-	*Sister Mary Ignatius Explains It All For You* *Vanya and Sonia and Masha and Spike*	
Wendy Wasserstein	1950-2006	*The Sisters Rosenweig* *The Heidi Chronicles**	
Beth Henley	1952-	*Crimes of the Heart** *The Miss Firecracker Contest*	
Tony Kushner	1956-	*Angels in America**	
Tracy Letts	1965-	*August: Osage County*	
Lin-Manuel Miranda	1980-	*In the Heights* *Hamilton**	

**Not only has Eugene O'Neill received more Pulitzer Prizes than any other playwright, he was also awarded the Nobel Prize in Literature in 1936, the only American playwright to ever receive this international honor as of 2020.

EASTERN THEATRE

One of the immediately visible appeals of any form of theatre is the lure of sound and color. Eastern theatre seems to have perfected this with larger-than-life costumes, expressive masks, life-like puppets, and a contagious, rhythmic beat.

Noh, the oldest form of Eastern theatre dating back to the fourteenth century, is deeply rooted in religion and ceremony. It is a combination of acting, dance, and music, rhythmically entwined in a strict form that has been passed to each new generation in a rigid training, which starts in an actor's childhood. The short plots generally deal with myths and legends, and the characters, like those of commedia dell'arte, are stock roles symbolized onstage by masks. Each Noh also has a kyogen, or comic interlude (remember the Greek satyr play?). The performance combines actors' gliding movements, chanting, and stomping in unison with a flute and drum accompaniment. The ultimate strength of the performance is in the fluid beauty of the combined movement, sound, and speech. It is the oldest form of theatre still performed today.

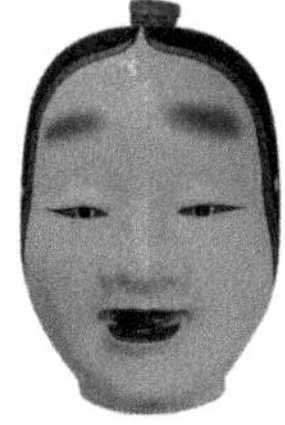

Noh Masks

Bunraku is a form of Japanese theatre that uses intricately hinged wooden puppets. Each elaborately costumed puppet stands four feet tall, and with moving fingers and facial expressions, it is no surprise that it takes three puppeteers for each figure. The puppeteers are masked in all black but are visible to the audience. However, once the elaborate story begins, they seem to disappear. This traditional Japanese puppet theatre first became popular in the seventeenth century.

The most influential of the Asian theatres is the Kabuki, which employs singing, dancing, and acting, just as its name would imply (ka = singing, bu = dancing, ki = acting). Originally produced by women, the newest of the three Eastern forms was an imitation of the Noh and the Bunraku. The plots are based on historical tales or stories about everyday life. Unlike the Noh, Kabuki actors do not wear masks. Instead, each is characterized by dramatic face paint, stylized movement, and elaborate costumes. Today, only men act in the plays. These men spend most of their lives studying their art, starting as children and remaining loyal actors until their deaths.

The Kabuki stage is a raised wooden platform, but because rhythmic stomping is such a prevalent part of the style, amplifying wooden sections are often laid on top of the stage. The hanamichi (flower path) is a raised passageway that extends from one corner of the stage through the audience. Here the actors make entrances and exits, often pausing midway for a pose or bit of dialogue. Like the Greeks, the Kabuki audience will hear narration and dialogue from a chorus of twelve to eighteen members. Each chorus member is uniformly dressed and carries a fan, adding to the beauty of the performance. The orchestra sits at the rear of the stage. They use drums, a flute, and a stringed instrument called a samisen. Dressed like the chorus, they add an almost burlesque quality to the performance, punctuating actors' entrances, exits, or emotional moments by clacking two wooden blocks together.

The kimono, the traditional, floor-length robe with draping sleeves, is worn by both male and female characters, each distinguished by a variance in color, fabric, or accessories. Stylized wigs are worn to add size and color, and unrealistic makeup is painted with brightly colored, sharply contrasting lines meant to show expression. At no point do the actors ever try to achieve realism, nor is that what the audience wants. Kabuki is fantasy storytelling. The actors' movements look more like dancing than acting, and their props are brought onstage by crew members dressed in all black with netting over their faces. Speeches are told with rhythmic musical accompaniment, or they may be told by several actors in unison or speaking in turn. It is theatre at its most ceremonial.

China boasts the Peking opera, a harmonious blend of song, dance, dialogue, and acrobatics. The subjects of the operas come from fiction, legend, and history. The superb costumes serve to enhance the performance, so they lack historical accuracy. Color is used to indicate rank and temperament. Originally acted by men, women were later introduced to the Chinese stage. After the establishment of the People's Republic in 1949, new plays were saturated with military propaganda. Only occasionally do new playwrights surface now.

NAME ______________________________ PERIOD ______ DATE ____________

RESTORATION AND LATER, AMERICAN, AND EASTERN THEATRE REVIEW

1. Where does the term "Restoration" come from?

2. What did the English Royal Patent do to change theatre?

3. ________________ wrote *The Country Wife* and is known for being a comic trendsetter, but ________________ is considered the master of comedy. The greatest actor of the Restoration was ________________, who also wrote plays and made innovative changes to lighting. His former girlfriend, ________________, was a feminist of sorts who was known for effectively playing women's and men's roles.

4. List the plays for which each of the following playwrights is famous:
   a. Richard Brinsley Sheridan
   b. Oliver Goldsmith
   c. Gilbert and Sullivan
   d. Oscar Wilde
   e. George Bernard Shaw

5. Theatre in America was outlawed until the mid 1700s when attitudes began to change. Early American theatres either produced plays from the __________ stage or borrowed plots from their plays to produce new ones. Americans wrote few plays of literary merit, and the introduction of __________ in the early twentieth century may have overshadowed the emergence of such greats as O'Neill and Wilder.

6. List three great American playwrights and some of their most outstanding works:

7. The oldest form of Japanese theatre is the __________, which is deeply rooted in religion and ceremony. ________________, a form of Japanese puppet theatre with Korean roots, uses large wooden puppets rather than live actors.

8. The newest and most influential form of Japanese theatre is the __________, which combines singing (_____), dancing (_____), and acting (_____), as its name implies. It was originally produced by __________ and was an imitation of the older two forms. It is characterized by ________________, ________________, and ________________. Today, only __________ perform in this form, and they dedicate their lives to the art.

9. Define kimono:

10. Define samisen:

THEATRE HISTORY TEST REVIEW CROSSWORD CLUES

ACROSS

1. Japanese "puppet" theatre
4. Commedia dell'arte performers travelled in ___________
9. Commedia dell'arte plays were basically ___________
13. Financed writers and actors and gave them credibility
15. Where "groundlings" viewed the plays
16. ___________ plays were based on stories from the Bible and saints' lives
18. Philosophical author of *Arms and the Man*
19. Greek actors
20. ___________ plays were based on Christ's final week
21. Rebellious Elizabethan writer
22. Marlowe's and Jonson's biggest rival
23. The first actor to step from the chorus
25. Means "goat song"_______________
27. Wrote *The Tragical History of Doctor Faustus*
30. O'Neill's *The* ___________ *Cometh*
33. Wrote *Antigone* and *Oedipus the King*
34. Shakespeare's patron queen
35. *The Crucible* playwright

DOWN

2. Japanese "singing, dancing, and acting" theatre
3. Twentieth century writer of cats, streetcars, and iguanas
5. A play of noble extravagance
6. The English Royal Patent ___________ theatre
7. Greeks honored this god with theatre
8. American ___________ almost overshadowed American stage
10. Commedia dell'arte ingenue's father
11. Elizabethans feared their presence onstage would cause immorality
12. Wrote *Medea*
14. Roman plays consisted of mimes, dancing, and ___________
17. Commedia dell'arte maidservant, the ___________
24. Wrote *Love for Love*
25. Ex-slave and Roman writer
26. Early American theatre plots were borrowed from the ___________
28. Greek "father of tragedy"
29. Penned *A Raisin in the Sun*
31. Place of performance recorded on stone tablet
32. Aristophanes wrote Greek ___________

NAME ______________________________ PERIOD ________ DATE ______________

THEATRE HISTORY TEST REVIEW CROSSWORD PUZZLE

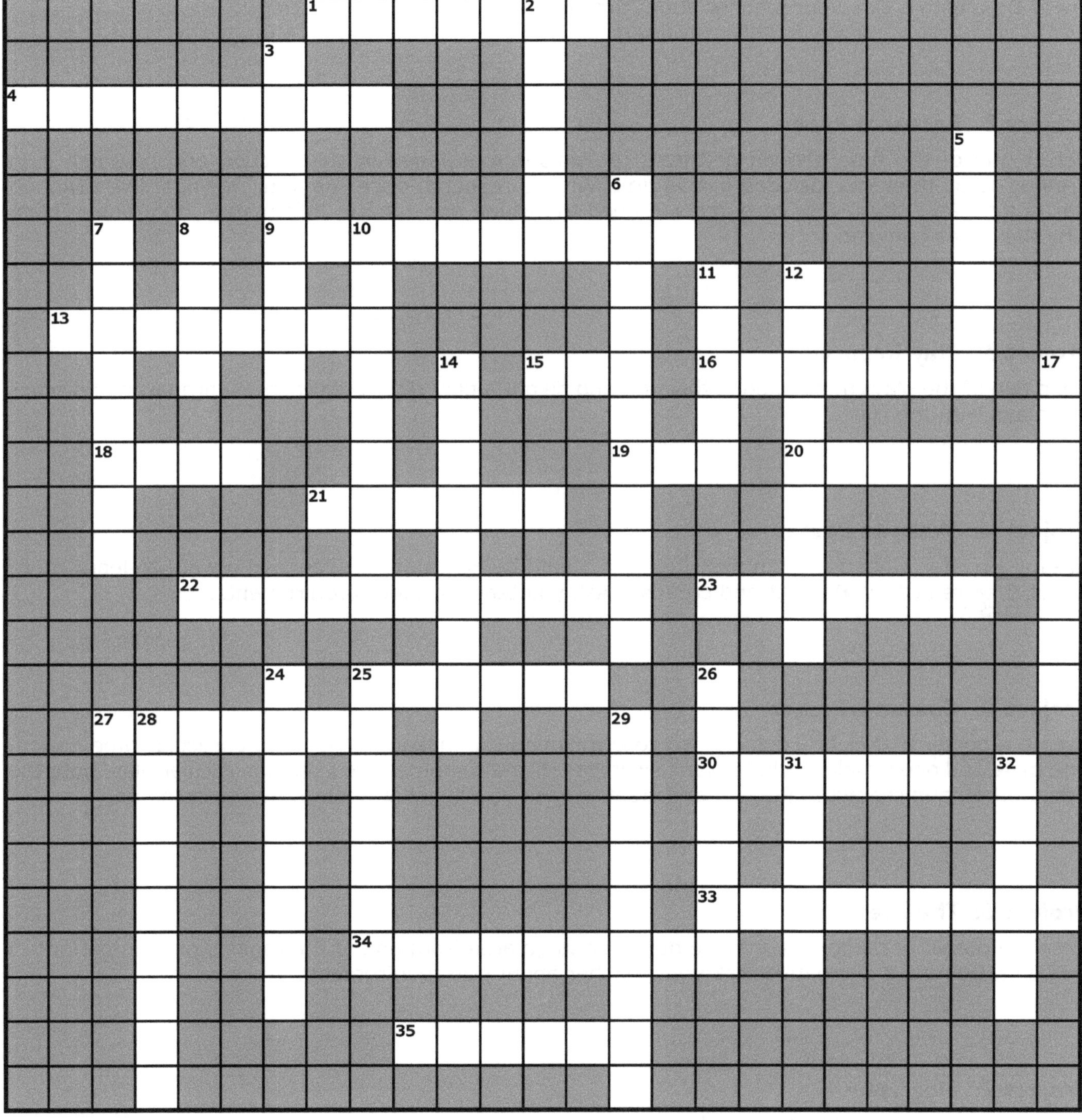

THEATRE HISTORY PROJECTS

Project 1: Performance

Select a play from any period other than modern. Read the play and then select a scene from the play to perform (monologue, duet, or group of three). Study the acting style of the period, the resources, the acting area, costumes, etc., and prepare your scene accordingly. Remember, in many periods women were not allowed to act. How will you deal with this without "getting into trouble with the law"? Be creative. Ask your teacher about time limits.

Project 2: Research Paper

Select one of the time periods or theatrical regions mentioned in this section and research it in greater detail than was included in this unit. Write a research paper on your findings. Even though this is a theatre class, your research will need to include non-theatre information, too, and explain why these are relevant.

Project 3: Play Reports

Read two of the plays mentioned in this unit and fill out a play report for each. Be prepared to discuss the plays with the class.

Project 4: Website Poster

Create a poster advertising ten websites that would be helpful to students who want to learn more about theatre history. Be neat and creative. Ask you teacher about requirements.

Project 5: Costume Poster

Create a poster that clearly depicts two costumes and the makeup styles of a particular time period, one male and one female. Include fabric swatches. If the costumes are from a particular play, note the title, author, and character. Be neat and creative. Ask your teacher about size requirements.

Project 6: Theatre

Create a poster or model of a theatre house or stage area from one of the regions or time periods in this unit. Be neat and creative. Ask your teacher about size requirements.

Project 7: Biography

Research any playwright of your choosing. Write a research paper on them and be prepared to present it to the class. Ask your teacher about length and other requirements.

CHAPTER 9
GAMES AND IMPROVISATION

DAILY BELL WORK—GAMES AND IMPROVISATION

IMPROVISATION

Understanding Improvisation
Improvisation Projects

NAME ______________________________ PERIOD ______ DATE __________

DAILY BELL WORK - GAMES AND IMPROVISATION

Answer each question as your teacher assigns it, using the space provided. Be sure to include the date.

1. Date: ______________

What is your favorite theatre game and why?

2. Date: ______________

What is your least favorite theatre game and why?

3. Date: ______________

Which game has provided you with the greatest theatrical insight and why?

4. Date: ______________

Why is it important for actors to play these games?

NAME ______________________________ PERIOD ________ DATE ____________

DAILY BELL WORK - GAMES AND IMPROVISATION

Answer each question as your teacher assigns it, using the space provided. Be sure to include the date.

5. Date: ________________

   How might theatre games benefit non-actors or other groups?

6. Date: ________________

   Why do young people sometimes clam up when it comes to playing the games, acting, or expressing themselves?

7. Date: ________________

   Actors are told to be uninhibited. That means they are to totally "let go" of their fears about how others may perceive them. Why is this important?

8. Date: ________________

   Tell how to play a game you know but that has not been played in this class. How might it help a young actor sharpen their skills?

NAME ______________________________ PERIOD ________ DATE ____________

DAILY BELL WORK - GAMES AND IMPROVISATION

Answer each question as your teacher assigns it, using the space provided. Be sure to include the date.

9. Date: ________________

   Create a plan for using improvisation or theatre games as a fundraiser. Include specific information such as the audience, the price of admission, and so on.

10. Date: ________________

    List as many "places" as you can for improvisation settings.

11. Date: ________________

    List a variety of stock characters for improvisations.

12. Date: ________________

    Can improvisation be practiced? Can someone learn to be an improvisational actor? Explain.

NAME ____________________ PERIOD ______ DATE __________

DAILY BELL WORK - GAMES AND IMPROVISATION

Answer each question as your teacher assigns it, using the space provided. Be sure to include the date.

13. Date: ______________

Paying attention to the instructions, listening to the other actors, and taking turns are vital to good improvisation. Explain.

14. Date: ______________

List some "situations" two characters might find themselves in for humorous improvisation.

15. Date: ______________

16. Date: ______________

IMPROVISATION

Improvisation, or improv, is a type of acting done without a script or rehearsal. An actor or group of actors is given a situation and sometimes characters, and they act it out spontaneously, making up the dialogue and action as they work their way to a solid conclusion. Part of what makes improvisation enjoyable to the audience is that they know and appreciate that the performance they are enjoying is being created especially for them.

There are several different types of improvisational games and activities actors can practice to improve their skills, and the number of scenes and types of characters is infinite. However, before you start, you need to know some of the basic ideas that make spontaneous scenes successful.

- **Define your character.** Take the director's prompt and do a quick character analysis before taking the stage: How do I walk and talk? How old am I? Do I have any odd habits?
- **Be a good listener.** Listen to the other actors onstage, because their lines are your cue lines, and if the scene lacks good teamwork, it will not be a success.
- **Know where you are.** Is your character at the mall, the zoo, the beach, or any other place that would enhance the scene? If there is not enough time to establish the location before beginning, work it into the skit as close to the beginning as possible. Then the imaginary location can become a part of the scene, giving you and the other actors more to go on.
- **Know the conflict.** Almost all scenes, improvisational or scripted, revolve around a conflict, and if improvisational actors are not clear on what it is, the scene will be confusing to the audience.
- **Identify the focus.** Sometimes beginning improv actors think their idea is better than what's happening in the main part of the scene, so they try to redirect the scene, which is the same as upstaging or stealing focus. Rather than upstaging, lend your energy to the area of main focus and help build the storyline.
- **Pay attention.** Whether playing a game or improvising a scene, remember the instructions: If there is a goal—and there almost always is—keep the goal in sight.
- **Establish relationships.** If relationships are not established by the teacher or director, clarify them early in the scene. This will help to clear the path for the conclusion.
- **Include plenty of action.** With no scenery or props, the actor has it within his power to "pretend" to possess anything he wishes! Good actors can use pantomime to make the audience believe they see a light saber or giant clown shoes.
- **Never say "no"** to wherever the scene is going. Saying "no" brings the scene to a sudden halt. If your scene partner says the grass just turned purple, then it did and you need to work with that instead of going against your partner. It keeps the scene moving toward the goal and tends to be funnier.
- **Find a conclusion.** Every scene needs to have a sense of completion, though when you are on the spot, this can be hard to do. Many improv troupes use bells and buzzers to end scenes that actors cannot seem to end on their own. You do not want to be buzzed out every time, so practice ending your own scenes.

NAME ______________________________ PERIOD ______ DATE ____________

UNDERSTANDING IMPROVISATION

Do you understand improvisation or improv?
Check your understanding by filling in the blanks on the following questions.

1. *Improvisation* or *improv* is a type of impromptu acting done without a ____________ or ____________.

2. The actors are given a situation to act spontaneously, making up the ____________ and ____________ as they work their way to a solid ____________.

3. It is important to quickly define one's character when doing improvisation. What are some things you might decide about characterization before taking the stage?

   ____

   ____

   ____

4. Improvisational actors must be good ____________. What others say onstage is important to each actor, because it may prompt them to say something useful to the outcome of the scene.

5. If there is not time to work it out before taking the stage, establish the ____________ of the scene as close to the beginning as possible, then the "surroundings" can be worked into the scene.

6. Know the ____________. Almost all scenes revolve around some struggle, and if you and your partners are not clear on exactly what it is, your scene will be confusing.

7. Pay attention. Whether playing a game or improvising a scene, remember the director's instructions: if there is a ____________, keep it in sight.

8. Establish relationships. If relationships are not established by the teacher or director, clarify them early in the scene. This will help to ____________.

9. Include plenty of ____________. With no scenery or props, the actor has it within their power to "pretend" to possess anything they wish! Good actors can use pantomime to make the audience believe they see anything.

10. Try to keep the scene in the ____________ rather than the ____________. Work with your partners instead of *against* them.

11. Every improvisation must have a ____________ that wraps up the events in the scene.

IMPROVISATION PROJECTS

Select one of the following projects to be completed and presented to the class on ______________. Each project must be neat and show strong effort. See your teacher for details or questions.

Project 1: Instructional Video

Make an instructional video with several other people to teach the class how to play a particular improvisational game or activity. The video should be well organized and cleanly pieced together.

Include:

- The title of the activity
- The source for the activity (where you found it)
- How many can play
- Materials needed
- Instructions and/or rules
- A successful sample of the activity
- How this particular activity is useful to theatre
- Credits

Project 2: Improvisation Notebook

Create an improvisation notebook that clearly instructs the reader how to play ten improvisation games or activities. The notebook should be neat and well organized. All of the material must be in the student's own words and format.

Each activity must include:

- The title of the activity
- The source for the activity (where you found it)
- How many can play
- Materials needed
- Instructions and/or rules
- How this particular activity is useful to theatre

Project 3: Fifty Famous Lines

Create a list of fifty famous lines, sayings, slogans, or lyrics for the "Whose Line Is Next?" game. The lines must be neatly typed and triple spaced on clean paper. Make sure the lines are appropriate for class.

Project 4: Fifty Pictures

Gather fifty pictures of people, animals, and items to be used in "The Picture Game." Cut them out neatly and mount each to a clean piece of paper slightly larger than the picture. Make sure the pictures are appropriate for class.

CHAPTER NINE NOTES:

CHAPTER 10

PLANNING FOR THE FUTURE

NAME ______________________________ PERIOD ________ DATE ____________

DAILY BELL WORK - PLANNING FOR THE FUTURE

Answer each question as your teacher assigns it, using the space provided. Be sure to include the date.

1. Date: ________________

   List as many jobs as you can think of in the field of theatre. Don't forget the ones backstage and in offices.

2. Date: ________________

   What are some non-theatre jobs that involve acting or good speaking skills?

3. Date: ________________

   What are some jobs that involve the skills learned in technical theatre?

4. Date: ________________

   Who do you know whose job is theatre related or uses theatre skills? Explain how they could benefit from using what you learned in this class.

NAME ______________________________ PERIOD ______ DATE ____________

DAILY BELL WORK - PLANNING FOR THE FUTURE

Answer each question as your teacher assigns it, using the space provided. Be sure to include the date.

5. Date: ________________

   Explain some of the things directors might look for on an actor's resume.

6. Date: ________________

   What might a director seek in an actor's headshot?

7. Date: ________________

   What are some ways an actor can get acting jobs?

8. Date: ________________

   Most actors have other jobs to pay bills while they try to find their big break. Which jobs would best accommodate actors' audition and rehearsal schedule?

NAME ______________________________ PERIOD ______ DATE __________

DAILY BELL WORK - PLANNING FOR THE FUTURE

Answer each question as your teacher assigns it, using the space provided. Be sure to include the date.

9. Date: ______________

   Agents rarely represent actors without experience, and it is hard to get experience without an agent. What would be a reasonable solution to this problem?

10. Date: ______________

    Often, good training can take the place of a lot of experience. What kinds of classes should actors seek?

11. Date: ______________

    List places actors can look to find information on agents.

12. Date: ______________

    Write an entry from an actor's journal on a typical day before getting their big break.

NAME ______________________________ PERIOD ______ DATE ____________

DAILY BELL WORK - PLANNING FOR THE FUTURE

Answer each question as your teacher assigns it, using the space provided. Be sure to include the date.

13. Date: ______________

    Write an entry from the same actor's journal on a typical day after getting their big break.

14. Date: ______________

    Athletes, musicians, and models often "break into acting" after building a name for themselves. Actors occasionally break into modeling and music, but rarely sports. What does this say about acting? What do you think of this practice?

15. Date: ______________

16. Date: ______________

WHY DO DRAMA?

Most students who take drama classes have no intention of becoming professional actors. Many are interested in acting because it is fun. They know they have a creative side and they wish to have an outlet to express themselves, but they do not dream of being on the red carpet someday. There are also those who do not really care for acting, but they must have a fine arts credit, and drama seems like the best solution. Many of these students eventually find that not only do they actually like the class, but also that they are talented. And yes, in our class there are also students with stars in their eyes who hope to act for a living one day. They are eager to learn all they can, be discovered, and become famous.

Whether you are one of the above students or somewhere in between, it is important to understand just why your theatre teacher asked you to do some activities. Believe it or not, acting like you are brushing your teeth in slow motion does serve a purpose. On a broader scale, it is also necessary to know and appreciate the reasons behind learning good articulation, speaking confidently and energetically, and using pauses effectively. Everything you have learned in this class translates to valuable life skills, regardless of your chosen career.

Think back on the various activities and lessons in this theatre class. In one column, list the activities for which you have a clear understanding of how they will one day benefit you. In the other, list those activities that remain unclear as to how they will impact your future. Discuss them in your class. Your fellow theatre students or your teacher may have a perspective on a particular activity that had not occurred to you.

I *understand* the potential future impact of these activities and lessons:

I *do not understand* the potential future impact of these activities and lessons:

NAME ______________________________ PERIOD ________ DATE ____________

THEATRE JOBS

There are many jobs one can do in the entertainment industry. Some are theatre jobs, such as acting, makeup, and technical work. Others are in the film, TV, and commercial industries. The following is a small sampling of the jobs one might seek.

STAGE CREW: There are many jobs within the stage crew. For example, grips move the scenery around during the show. The props manager buys or creates the many props used in the show and makes sure that they are always placed where they are needed. Sometimes the members of the stage crew even build and paint the set, but some theatres have construction crews who do this. All of these jobs and many more are overseen by the technical director, who runs all of the technical aspects of the show and works in the interest of the director and the stage manager, who handles the show from backstage.

Imagine you are on the crew for a children's comedy about Aladdin. Explain how your show's set and props would differ from an adult drama about the same character.

____

____

____

LIGHTING: There are many people on the lighting team. A designer designs the lights, including where to hang which instruments, what gel color to put in the instrument frame, when to bring lights up and down during the show, and what intensity and effects to use. Light technicians hang and gel the instruments and take care of them throughout the show. The light board operator runs the lights during the show. Spotlight operators maneuver the lights used to follow actors during certain scenes.

How can lighting be used to establish the mood of a play? Give examples.

____

____

____

SOUND: The sound crew has quite a few responsibilities. Depending on the show's requirements, there may be as few as a single sound crew member or as many as ten. The sound crew is responsible for all of the microphones, the crew's headsets used to communicate during the show, and all of the sound effects used during the show. They are also responsible for any background music that might be used. Most importantly, they monitor the sound levels during the show to make sure that the quality stays good.

How could sound effects add realism to a scene about a campfire on a starry night?

____

____

____

NAME ______________________________ PERIOD ______ DATE __________

COSTUMES AND MAKEUP: The costumers and makeup artists work very closely with the director and the technical director to provide a style, theme, and overall look that is congruent with the rest of the production. Larger theatres have a designer and a seamstress (and sometimes several of each). Smaller theatres rely on costume rental houses to provide them with appropriate costumes. In the world of professional theatre, talented artisans create complex designs, which can truly complete the actor's characterization.

Color is a very important part of any show's overall design, but especially when it comes to costuming. Explain how color can be symbolic within the costume design of a show.

____

____

____

PUBLICITY: The person or crew responsible for the promotion of a show has a huge job. They must coordinate news releases and advertisements. They must create a schedule in which pictures can be taken in costume for publicity and programs but without disturbing the most important phase of the rehearsal process—the technical rehearsals. Posters must be designed and printed and visibly hung in appropriate places and tickets must be printed and sold. Programs have to be designed and printed, and often advertisers purchase ad space in these. Many theatres have a phone line to be maintained and a mailing list for sending out flyers. Finally, theatres often have reserved seating or special offers on season tickets. All of this is maintained by the publicity crew.

Discuss the pros and cons of general admission seating at a lower rate versus reserved seating at a higher rate.

____

____

____

CHOREOGRAPHER: Makes up the dance routines for any show that involves dancing.

SPECIAL EFFECTS MANAGER: Creates and monitors special effects for shows and is responsible for the safety of the actors and the audience.

HOUSE MANAGER: Takes charge of the audience area of the theatre before, during, and after performances, including managing the ushers and concessions and attending to the general comfort of the audience.

WRITER: Creates the script.

MUSICAL DIRECTOR: In musical theatre, this person is in charge of bringing all of the musical elements together to support the goals of the director.

STAGE COMBAT DIRECTOR: Choreographs the more physical part of the show and monitors actors for safety. Stage combat can include fist fighting, wrestling, swordplay, or simply a trip or kick. It is very complex and requires extensive training.

STUNTPERSON: Used mainly in film and TV, the stuntperson, who has received special training, doubles for an actor to perform physically challenging or dangerous tasks.

CAMERAPERSON: Operates the camera for film and video.

NAME ______________________________ PERIOD ________ DATE ____________

ACTING OPPORTUNITIES

There are many careers that involve acting or acting skills that offer reasonable incomes. Granted, most actors would like to "hit the big time" and become stars. However, many take on more stable jobs to pay bills while seeking their big break on the side. Others who love acting but decide to keep it a hobby while building another career altogether.

The following list of careers are typical jobs many actors will do at one time or another. Some offer lucrative salaries; some do not. Discuss the jobs as a class. Do you know what is meant by each? If not, take a moment to find out. Which jobs appeal to you? Which seem more like fun than work? Which seem more like work than fun? Which are easy and which are difficult? Can you see yourself doing any of these? After you have discussed the acting alternatives, answer the questions below.

______TV Commercial Actor	______Dinner Theatre Actor	______Voice-over Talent
______Movie Actor	______Murder Mystery Actor	______Cartoon Voice
______Newscaster	______Play Actor	______Audio Book Voice
______Disc Jockey	______Children's Theatre Actor	______Educational Video Actor
______Model	______Public Speaker	______Community Theatre Actor
______Movie Extra	______Master of Ceremonies	______Stand-up Comedian
______Industrial Video Actor	______Improv Player	______Motivational Speaker

1. In the spaces to the left of the job, rank them in the order of preference with 1 being the most preferred and 21 being the least preferred. Then think about your ranking. What motivated your choices? Was it ability, salary, or personal enjoyment? Maybe it was something else. Explain your reasoning below.

2. Can you think of other jobs that involve acting that are not on the list?

3. Which jobs do you think are hardest to get into? Why?

4. Which jobs do you think would offer a part-time actor the most flexibility to attend auditions and rehearsals? Why?

NAME ______________________________ PERIOD ________ DATE ______________

NON-THEATRE JOBS

There are many jobs that involve the skills you learn in this class but have nothing or very little to do with theatre. Many involve being in front of large groups of people on a daily basis. Some involve being "a character" or being emotional. Others require the ability to move or speak as actors do. In small groups, discuss the following questions and write your answers in the space provided.

1. What are some of the primary skills students learn in this class? Be specific.

______________ ______________ ______________

______________ ______________ ______________

______________ ______________ ______________

2. List as many jobs as you can think of that involve any of these skills.

______________ ______________ ______________

______________ ______________ ______________

______________ ______________ ______________

______________ ______________ ______________

______________ ______________ ______________

3. Pick one of the jobs listed above and explain specifically how theatre skills might help someone in this particular career.

4. Can you think of some jobs that do not involve any theatre skills?

5. Write an advertisement for this theatre class explaining the benefits for people interested in all types of careers. Be creative!

NETWORKING

Networking is a valuable skill to learn as you begin to plan your future. Whether you're working on skills to start a career or enrolling in a college or trade school, the people you meet along the way are good resources to help you move forward. Working to stay in touch with your contacts and developing a solid base of other resources will help you succeed. Keep a contact list of people, businesses, and places that could benefit your future. You never know what kind of contacts you might need in the future, so think broadly and develop a place where you keep information for a broad range of resources.

WHO

Accompanists
Acting teachers
Advertising Agents
Animal trainers
Casting directors
Choral directors
Choreographers
Combat trainers
Costumers
Dance instructors
Dialect instructor
Gymnasts
Hair stylists
Headshot photographers
Headshot printers
Jugglers
Magicians
Makeup artists
Marketing firms
Mimes
Musicians
News agencies
Painters/artists
Photographers
Printers
Production companies
Public relations companies
Public speaking organizations
Resume companies
Sound companies
Speech teachers
Voice teachers

WHAT

Accessories
Alterations
Backdrops
Construction (scenery)
Drapery maintenance
Ear pieces and microphones
Floor maintenance
General maintenance
House maintenance
Karaoke rentals
Lighting maintenance
Lighting rentals
Makeup supplies
Masks
Program/poster
Recording (voice over)
Scenery
Scripts
Sound effects
Sound systems
Tickets

WHERE

Amateur theatres
Children's theatre
Colleges/universities
Comedy clubs
Convention center
Festivals
Opera production studios
Professional theatres
Radio stations
Theatre camps

WORKING AS AN ACTOR

Anyone wishing to work seriously and make a living as an actor needs to know exactly what tools are required for the job. Just as an artist needs canvas and paints, there are many things an actor needs to get the job done.

The first preparation anyone needs for any career is education. For actors, education means training. Many colleges and universities offer degrees in theatre or musical theatre. One benefit of attending college is that one can select both a major and a minor. Many theatre majors select a minor in the career with which they will "pay bills." Also, attending college gives actors excellent training in a working environment. Theatre majors must participate in the shows, the greatest hands-on training available.

Versatile actors train for the broadest of possibilities, covering all of their bases. They take voice and dance lessons to prepare for musical theatre. Even those who have no faith in their own musical and dance abilities should consider this, as they will learn to grasp voice and movement concepts not always taught in acting classes. Many realize that they are better than they thought and are quite trainable. Others simply take the classes hoping to network with other actors, learn their limitations, or have skills to put on their resumes.

There are several types of acting classes as well. There are classes that specifically deal with commercial acting and others that deal with movie acting. Many classes have beginner, intermediate, and advanced levels. Some are taught privately and some in groups. At the college level, acting classes are more specifically focused. Voice and diction classes teach actors proper speaking techniques. Movement classes deal with the actor's body and how it relates to the character, the environment, and the situation. There are even classes that deal specifically with classical acting.

Beyond training, actors must obtain the physical tools of the trade: the professional headshot and resume. A headshot is an 8 x 10" "head and shoulders" photo of the actor with their name along the top or bottom. Some still require this in black and white; others now prefer color. Just like fashion, the trend of these photos changes with each passing year, the specific acting industry being sought, and even geographical location. For example, some jobs seek a glamorous look, while others seek a more relaxed look. It may be wise to consult a few professional actors and photographers in your area before making an investment. The actor will also need a resume that tells as much as possible about the actor without being cumbersome. While an actor gets fifty or a hundred headshots printed at a time, they might only print ten resumes, as they will want to update it after each job. The resume is generally attached back-to-back with the headshot. At auditions, this allows the casting director to either separate the two pieces or easily flip one over to view the other.

Now the actor has the tools necessary to seek an agent. Talent agents are people who work for the actor to get auditions. Once the actor auditions for the job, the agent negotiates the contract and acts as liaison between the actor and the producer or director. The agent works for a percentage of the actor's pay, so it is in their best interest to negotiate the highest possible pay. Some actors never get agents, but because many directors will not hire a non-represented actor, most seek professional representation. A good agent can turn a part-time actor into a full-time professional.

RESUMES AND HEADSHOTS

Resumes and headshots are the actor's calling card. Without impressive credentials, it is unlikely that they will ever get their foot in the door of an audition. As with any other profession, the acting industry has standards, but those standards vary depending on the market. The market may include the geographic region, the type of acting job, and the job's physical requirements.

The sample resume in this section is for an Austin, Texas, actor seeking commercial and film work. That is why commercials are listed first. Stage actors would list their stage experience first. Do not be discouraged if you cannot write something for every category. Many actors spend years building their resumes. Some wonderful books and online resources are available to help you format yours so that it looks professional and fits your market. There are also many professionals who create resumes for a living. While they charge for this service, the results are worth the investment, especially if you hire someone with experience formatting entertainment resumes.

Name—Use the name you want people to remember. For example, if you are Jonathan Smith but you only go by John Smith, then use the latter name. Many actors use their nicknames, and some choose stage names. While stage names are fun, they are becoming less common. The most recent trend is wholesome and natural, and that even applies to one's name. Names that sound pretend have no real theatrical appeal.

Some actors will use easy versions of difficult names. For example, Mikaela Ricardini might choose to go by Miki Richards, simply because it is easier for casting directors to pronounce. Androgynous names help actors get extra work if they can easily pull off gender non-specific roles. Pricilla might choose to go by Presley, or Coby James might go by CJ. And names with a strong cultural tilt might not work as well as culturally generic ones. One young actor was getting called to auditions for Russian characters because of her Russian name. But she wasn't being hired because she didn't look the part and couldn't speak the language or even fake the accent. She experimented with a more generic name, and suddenly, she was being called for a larger variety of auditions, and she began booking roles.

Actors should never feel pressured to adopt stage names. It's a personal choice, and it should be one you consider carefully. If you choose to use a name other than your own, check with your bank before your first paying job to determine if you need to do anything special to deposit checks!

Address, Phone, and Email—If you do not have an agent, you will use your own contact information on all printed and electronic materials. After securing an agent, you will use your name but your agent's contact information on your headshot and resume.

Hair and Eyes—Generally you will include some information about your appearance, such as hair and eye color. You may also need to include sizes or measurements, height and weight, and any unusual physical characteristics of particular interest, such as "professional bodybuilder." However, until you have an agent and for safety reasons, include only your hair and eye color.

Training, Special Skills, and Professional Organizations—List each class and workshop individually. If the class is school-related, do not include the name of the school until the college level, but always include the teachers' names. Training is generally considered as important as experience and is easy to get. Special skills are those things you can do that many others cannot, such as sports (be specific) and tricks. They may include ballroom dancing, volleyball, martial arts, juggling, and speaking Japanese. Professional organizations may include any organization related to your particular fields of interest as they are relevant to your career. For example, Screen Actors Guild is certainly worthy of being included in your resume, but chess club is not.

Headshots are a bit more difficult to manufacture. You may go to a professional headshot photographer. While this is the most expensive option, it's likely to be the best if you are in a competitive market. One way to reduce the cost is to hire a professional who will give you a better rate by coming to the school and taking a dozen pictures of each serious acting student.

Another budget-friendly option is to find a friend who is a good photographer and create homemade headshots. Find an indoor location with good lighting and a solid background and pose naturally in portrait mode. Do basic editing to enhance the quality of the photo; however, do not change the person in the photo. Do not use filters, and do not try to make the person look better, thinner, younger, or with a clearer complexion. The only exception would be to erase something temporary, like a bruise, blemish, or hair out of place. But making someone with severe acne look like they have a clear complexion is unacceptable because it is not the truth. Now, add your name to the top or bottom so that it is easy to read. Keep the font simple. A busy font will frustrate casting directors and agents!

RESUME FORM

Name: ______________________________

Address: ______________________________

Phone: ____________________ Email: ____________________

Hair color: ______________ Eye Color: ______________

COMMERCIALS

Role	Title or Product	Product/Production Company

FILM/TELEVISION

Role	Title	Production Company/Director

PLAYS

Role	Title	Theatre or Company

MUSICALS

Role	Title	Theatre or Company

MISCELLANEOUS EXPERIENCE

Role or Job	Event Title	Company

TRAINING

____

____

SPECIAL SKILLS

____

____

PROFESSIONAL ORGANIZATIONS

____

SAMPLE HEADSHOT

A sample headshot for a female commercial actor in the 14-22 year age range in Dallas.

Rachel DeRouen

Photo credit: Arthur Bryan Marroquin, ABM Photography.

SAMPLE FICTIONAL RESUME

Rachel DeRouen

Studio Talent, Inc.
123 Main • Dallas, Texas 75555
972-555-1234
Studiotalent@fiction.com

Blue eyes • Blonde hair

COMMERCIALS

Principal non-speaking	Visionmart	PLQ & Associates
Student	Republican Promotional	GH Productions
Principal speaking	Burger Hut	TRU Productions

FILM/TELEVISION

Witness	Police Academy Instructional	Bradore College Police Association
Extra/Diner	*Case of the Missing Piano*	Robert Boyce, director
Extra/Cheerleader	*The Special Game*	Clueless Productions
Debbie Charles	*A Walk in the Rain*	Gifford Productions

THEATRE

Stella Kowalski	*A Streetcar Named Desire*	Lake Bend High School
Doreen	*Tartuffe*	Bradore College Junior Camp
Tansy	*The Nerd*	Theatre Off the Wall
Florence Unger	*The Odd Couple, Female Version*	Lakeside Teens
Katherine	*Taming of the Shrew*	Spotlight Productions

MUSICALS

Auntie Mame	*Mame*	Spotlight Productions
Assistant Director	*Annie Get Your Gun*	Spotlight Productions
Wicked Witch	*The Wizard of Oz*	Bradore College Junior Camp

MISCELLANEOUS EXPERIENCE

Three years of experience singing telegrams, Blue Bunny Singers
Two seasons as "Genie," State Fair
One season as "ballerina," Children's Tent, State Fair

TRAINING

In second year of Associate of Fine Arts degree program, Bradore College, acting scholarship. Receiving specialized training in acting (Jim Caldwell) and stage makeup (Brodie Ballard).
Voice-over training by QZP Productions (Hugh Lory and Betty Simmons).
Seven years ballet with Dallas Children's Ballet and Dallas Choral Ballet.

SPECIAL SKILLS

Voice-over, various dialects/accents, fluent in French and Spanish, experienced ballet dancer, can juggle and do illusions, softball, ice hockey, karate, dirt bike riding, various forms of stunt work. Member SAG, AFTRA, Actors Equity.

CAREER PROJECTS

Project 1: Interview

Select someone who is either in the field of theatre or uses theatre skills on the job. Ask them as many questions as you like, but for this project, you must ask at least ten theatre-related questions. Prepare your questions before you go in for the interview and be as professional as possible. You may record the interview and present it to the class or write the results in essay form.

Project 2: Research Paper

Select one of the careers mentioned in this section and research it. Write a research paper on your findings as the career relates to theatre.

Project 3: Guest Speaker

Arrange a guest speaker for the class for a twenty-minute question-and-answer session about their career and how it either relates to theatre or uses theatre skills. Be sure to prepare a complimentary introduction of your guest to the class. Have the class prepare questions in advance, and make sure that the speaking engagement is cleared through both your teacher and the school first.

Project 4: Website Poster

Create a poster advertising ten websites that would be helpful to students who may be trying to find jobs in theatre or alternative acting careers. Be neat and creative, and make sure everything is visible. Use caution about the appropriateness of the websites you advertise.

NAME ______________________________ PERIOD ______ DATE ____________

YOUR FUTURE IN THEATRE CROSSWORD PUZZLE

Complete the crossword puzzle about theatre as a part of your future. The answers to the clues come from the worksheets in this section. Eliminate spaces, hyphens, and apostrophes from your puzzle answers.

ACROSS

1. The group of people responsible for music, microphones, and sound effects during a show
4. The 8 x 10″ photo of the actor
7. The person who takes care of the show from backstage
9. Stagehands who move scenery during a show
10. The stage crew member who is responsible for props
12. The light __________ operator runs lights during the show
14. The person who is in charge of the "artistry" of the lights
15. Takes the actors' places for dangerous or difficult tasks

DOWN

2. Creates the dance routines for a musical or dance
3. __________ may be created by a seamstress or rented
5. In most high schools, students apply their own __________ rather than hiring an artist
6. The ______ manager takes care of the audience's needs
8. The first thing an actor must obtain before starting a career
11. The document that "sells" the actor, explaining education, experience, and skills
13. The person who gets the professional actor auditions and negotiates contracts

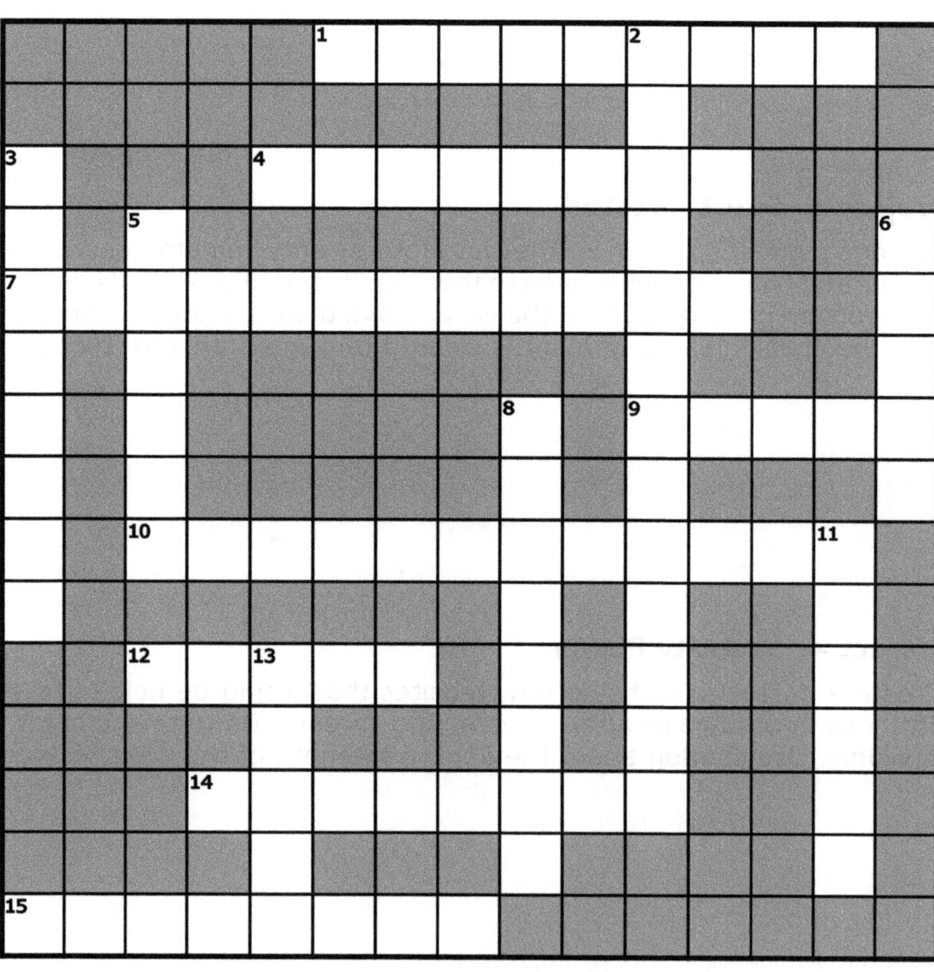

BIBLIOGRAPHY

1. Brater, Enoch and Phyllis Hartnoll. *The Theatre: A Concise History*. Third Edition. Thames and Hudson: London, Great Britain. 1998.

2. Britannia: America's gateway to the British Isles, 1689–1901 AD. Copyright © 2000 Britannia.com LLC. Delaware.

3. Galileo Timeline. Rice University. Copyright © 1995 Albert Van Heldon. Houston, Texas.

4. History for Kids. Portland State University. Copyright © 2002, 2003 Dr. Karen E. Carr. Portland, Oregon.

5. Theatre History.com. http://www.theatrehistory.com. Copyright © 2002 Theatre History.com. Burlington, Massachusetts.

6. History World. http://www.historyworld.net. Copyright © Historyworld Ltd. Part of the National Grid for Learning.

7. ORB: The Online Reference Book for Medieval Studies. Copyright © 1995–2002 Laura V. Blanchard and Carolyn Schriber. Rhodes College and Western Michigan University. Kalamazoo, Michigan.

8. Pettengill, R. and Lisa Abel (editor). *Theatre Art in Action*. NTC/Contemporary Publishing Company: Chicago, Illinois. 2001.

9. Reshafim, André Dollinger. *Introduction to the History and Culture of Pharaonic Egypt*. Copyright © 2000 André Dollinger Reshafim.

10. Schanker, Harry H. and Katharine Anne Ommanney. *The Stage and the School*. Eighth Edition. Glencoe/MacMillan McGraw Hill: New York, New York. 1998.

ABOUT THE AUTHOR

Suzi Zimmerman was the youngest of three children and, admittedly, a bit of a troublemaker. Her siblings were good at sports and music, but she seemed to be flailing. She knew she was creative and loved to perform, but her community focused mainly on sports and music. Those who lacked a place tended to become bored, which led to unacceptable behavior.

She finally discovered theatre, but only because it was offered at the high school level. It was then that she vowed to fight for more accessible performance opportunities for all levels. After college, she founded a local theatre troupe, which eventually became a community theatre, fulfilling her dream of bringing performance opportunities to all. After twenty years in public education, she is now a full-time writer, artist, and businessperson.

Zimmerman has acted professionally in film and on the stage. She is the spokesperson for and director of New Hope Foundation, a nonprofit in northern Texas working to improve the lives of underprivileged families. She is married with five children, two of whom are successful in the film industry.

A STUDENT-FRIENDLY, TEACHER-FRIENDLY WORKBOOK

Study units for an entire year of classroom activity

1. GETTING STARTED
2. EVALUATION
3. SCENE WORK
4. ACTING
5. CHARACTERIZATION
6. PUBLICITY
7. PLAY PRODUCTON
8. THEATRE HISTORY
9. GAMES AND IMPROV
10. FUTURE PLANNING

A 36-WEEK CLASSROOM-TESTED PROGRAM

MERIWETHER PUBLISHING
A division of Pioneer Drama Service, Inc.